MW00573403

RUSSIAN BALLET MASTER

The Memoirs of Marius Petipa

MARIUS PETIPA
A caricature by S. and N. Legat

RUSSIAN BALLET MASTER

The Memoirs of

MARIUS PETIPA

EDITED BY
LILLIAN MOORE

TRANSLATED BY HELEN WHITTAKER

DANCE BOOKS
9 CECIL COURT LONDON W.C.2.

THIS IS AN UNABRIDGED REPUBLICATION
OF THE EDITION FIRST PUBLISHED IN 1958
BY A. & C. BLACK LTD., LONDON.

ENGLISH TRANSLATION
© 1958 A. & C. BLACK LTD.

CONTENTS

PAGE

INTRODUCTION viii

PREFACE xv

CHAPTER

I A DANCER'S CHILDHOOD 1

II ACROSS THE ATLANTIC AND BACK 8

III A DUEL IN SPAIN 14

IV MY ARRIVAL IN ST PETERSBURG 22

V AN INSULT TO ANDREYANOVA 27

VI FANNY ELSSLER AND THE EMPEROR 31

VII BERLIN AND PARIS 36

VIII A GAME OF CHESS 44

IX THE DAUGHTER OF PHARAOH 49

X FRUITFUL YEARS 56

XI THE COLONEL-OF-THE-ARTS 66

XII REFORMS AND INTRIGUES 75

XIII TROUBLES AND TRIBUTES 85

BALLETS AND PRODUCTIONS BY MARIUS
PETIPA, IN CHRONOLOGICAL ORDER 95

REVIVALS AND PRODUCTIONS OF FOREIGN
BALLETS, STAGED BY MARIUS PETIPA 101

DANCES STAGED BY MARIUS PETIPA IN
OPERAS 103

ILLUSTRATIONS

1. Marius Petipa, a caricature by S. and N. Legat . *Frontispiece*
2. Jean Petipa (*New York Public Library*) . . xiv
3. Marius Petipa (*New York Public Library*) . . . xiv
4. Madame Lecomte in *La Sylphide* (*Harvard Theatre Collection*) xv
5. Marie Guy-Stéphan (*New York Public Library*) . . 16
6. Carlotta Grisi and Lucien Petipa in *Le Diable à Quatre* (*New York Public Library*) 17
7. Carlotta Grisi and Lucien Petipa in *Giselle* (*Collection of Lillian Moore*) 17
8. The "Guitar" Carriage (*New York Public Library*) . . 22
9. Fanny Elssler dancing the "Pas Stratégique" in *Catarina* (*New York Public Library*) 23
10. Fanny Elssler in *La Sylphide* (*Collection of Lillian Moore*) . 23
11. Elena Andreyanova (Cia Fornaroli Collection, *New York Public Library*) 26
12. Elena Andreyanova, a caricature by an anonymous artist (*New York Public Library*) 26
13. Elena Andreyanova and Emile Gredelu (*New York Public Library*) 26
14. Yrca Matthias (*Harvard Theatre Collection*) . . . 27
15. Fanny Elssler in *The Swiss Milkmaid* (*Austrian National Library*) 32
16. Fanny Elssler in *Danse Cosaque* (*Collection of Lillian Moore*) 33
17. Fanny Elssler in *La Tarentule* (*Victoria and Albert Museum*) . 33
18. Leontine Fay Volnys (*New York Public Library*) . . 36
19. Laure Milla (*New York Public Library*) . . . 36
20, 21. Marie Petipa at the time of her appearances in Paris (*New York Public Library*) 36
22. Marie Petipa and Felix Kschessinski in *La Diable à Quatre* (*Collection of Hope Sheridan*) . . . 37
23. Carolina Rosati in *Le Corsair* (*Collection of Lillian Moore*) . 44
24. Martha Muravieva (*New York Public Library*) . . 44
25. Ekaterina Vazem (*Collection of Lillian Moore*) . . 44
26. Marius Petipa in *Faust* 45
27. Marius Petipa in *The Daughter of Pharaoh* . . . 45
28. Marius Petipa in middle age (*New York Public Library*) . 45
29. *The Sleeping Beauty*, the Prologue from the Royal Ballet Production (*Edward Mandinian*) 64
30. Carlotta Brianza, who created *The Sleeping Beauty* (*Harvard Theatre Collection*) 65
31. Margot Fonteyn in *The Sleeping Beauty* (*Richard Dormer*) . 65

vi

32. Pierina Legnani as Odette in *Swan Lake* . . . 80
33. Alicia Alonso as Odette in *Swan Lake* (*Walter E. Owen*) . 80
34. Maria Tallchief, Yvonne Mounsey and Patricia Wilde in the New York City Ballet's production of *Swan Lake* (*G. B. L. Wilson*) 81
35. *The Nutcracker*, a scene from George Balanchine's production for the New York City Ballet (*Fred Fehl*) . 81
36. Margot Fonteyn and Michael Somes in the Royal Ballet's production of *Swan Lake* (*Baron*) . . . 82
37, 38. Solianikov and Rosinante in *Don Quixote*, and Alexander Gorsky; two caricatures by S. and N. Legat (*New York Public Library*) 83
39. Marius Petipa's daughter Marie, with Pavel Gerdt in *The Seasons* (*New York Public Library*) . . . 86
40. Alexander Golovine's design for *The Magic Mirror*, Act 3, Scene 6 86
41. Marius Petipa, aged ninety (*New York Public Library*) . 87

The Playbill on page 13 shows the programme of the first appearance in New York of Marius and Jean Petipa, 29th October 1839 (*Harvard Theatre Collection*)

ACKNOWLEDGEMENTS

WE are deeply grateful to the friends who have helped us so much in the preparation of this book. Mr Anatole Chujoy, editor of *Dance News*, not only read the manuscript, but compared it with the original, generously placing at our disposal all the vast resources of his authoritative knowledge of Russian ballet and the Russian language. Miss Mary Clarke, Miss Phyllis DuBois, Miss Anahide Sarantchof and Mr Ivor Guest made many valuable suggestions.

Miss Genevieve Oswald, Curator of the Dance Collection of the New York Public Library, was helpful not only in the preparation of the notes, but also in the difficult task of selecting the illustrations, the great majority of which were found in the rich collection she has done so much to assemble. We are grateful also to Dr William Van Lennep and Miss Mary Reardon of the Harvard Theatre Collection, to Miss Hope Sheridan, who kindly loaned a rare music cover, and to Ing. Herbert A. Mansfeld, of Vienna, who assisted in obtaining illustrations from the Oesterreichische Nationalbibliothek.

INTRODUCTION

BY LILLIAN MOORE

MARIUS PETIPA was a great choreographer, and more than a choreographer. As virtual dictator of the Russian ballet, he moulded its course for many years, and may even be said to have created the style of classical dancing still known as Russian. His renown is undisputed, and his work lives not only in the pages of dance history, but in the active ballet repertoire. The three magnificent works on which he collaborated with Tschaikovsky—*The Sleeping Beauty*, *Swan Lake*, and *The Nutcracker*—are permanent monuments to his genius. Although their creator has been dead for half a century, they still form the cornerstone of ballet repertoire, and are danced, in one form or another, all over the world.

No one would have been more surprised than Petipa himself, if he could have looked into the future and seen that his work would be more universally appreciated, fifty years after his death, than it was even during his greatest period of creative activity and success. The recognition given Petipa's ballets today is based upon the fact that they have withstood drastic tests: the passage of time, transplanting from one country to others of vastly different cultural backgrounds, and the devastating effects of several different choreographic revolutions.

In his last years, Petipa was an embittered and disillusioned man. He felt that he had been put on the shelf while he was still full of energy and ideas, and that even the work he had accomplished was being systematically destroyed. The turn of the century was a time of ferment in the theatrical world of St Petersburg. Young painters, musicians, dancers and choreographers were eager to experiment with new forms, and the familiar pattern of Petipa's work was considered antiquated and outmoded. The triumphant progress of the young revolutionaries who were to form the nucleus of the Diaghilev Ballet, and to bring Russian art to western Europe, is well known. It was inevitable that the strength of the rising tide should force Petipa's work temporarily into the background, and that it should suffer a long period of neglect.

In the past decade, however, through the excellent productions of his masterpieces by the Royal Ballet, through the direct inspiration he has provided to such choreographers as Balanchine and Ashton, and even through the gradual dissemination of fragments of his choreographic treasure all over the globe, his work has gained a place which seems extraordinarily permanent and secure in the most ephemeral of arts.

Petipa wrote these memoirs in a very dark hour, in 1905, when he was a disheartened and discouraged old man. His last ballet, *The Magic Mirror*, had been a disastrous failure. His assistant and protégé, Lev Ivanov, whom he had hoped would succeed him as Ballet Master of the St Petersburg Imperial Theatres, had died four years before. Alexander Gorsky, a young choreographer with whose experiments Petipa had little sympathy, seemed to be usurping his position. Michel Fokine, whose early work Petipa was to admire and encourage, had not yet produced *The Vine*, given at a pupils' performance in 1906, at just about the time when these memoirs were first coming off the press.

In an attempt to justify his position and call attention to the length and scope of his distinguished career as a dancer and choreographer, Petipa decided to write his memoirs. He was eighty-six years old. Probably he dictated them (in French, doubtless, for after nearly sixty years in St Petersburg he still had not learned to express himself fluently in Russian), for his tone, even in the Russian in which they were published, seems casual and conversational, and he often skips rather abruptly from one subject and one period to another, as one might do in talking. In the last pages, where he speaks of the new Director of the Imperial Theatres, Teliakovsky, who has taken away all his power over his beloved ballet company, one can almost hear the echoes of his furious, trembling voice.

Elderly people often recall most vividly the days of their early youth, and Petipa was no exception. His childhood in Brussels, his adventures in Bordeaux and Madrid, his brief excursion to America and his first journey to Russia are all recalled in colourful detail. So are his début performances in St Petersburg and Moscow, and his impressions of the great Viennese ballerina Fanny Elssler.

But when he reaches his own period of glory, in the days when he produced *The Sleeping Beauty*, *Swan Lake*, and *Raymonda*, he disappoints us by skipping over it as though it were too well known to need discussion: " . . . During those never-to-be-forgotten seventeen years of Vsevolojsky's management, every one of my ballets was successful . . ." And he merely lists them!

Absorbed by his anxiety to justify himself in the eyes of his audience, he brings out letter after letter, some of them of genuine interest, like the one from Tschaikovsky concerning the composition of the score for *The Sleeping Beauty*, and others which are pitiful little scraps of tribute from dancers like Enrichetta Grimaldi and Maria Gorshenkova, who today would be entirely forgotten except for the fact that they once appeared in Petipa's ballets!

Nevertheless, these sometimes pathetic pages give us an insight into Petipa's character and genius that it might be impossible to gain from any other source. For fifty years, he enjoyed a security such as few dancers or choreographers have ever experienced. The sheer volume of his accomplishment, in the production of ballets, the training and development of dancers, and the foundation of an entire school of ballet, the Russian (a combination of technical elements from the French and Italian schools, plus indigenous factors contributed by the Russian dancers themselves), was stupendous.

Nevertheless, the end of his career found him full of doubts and disillusionment.

In these memoirs, even in the pages devoted to his triumphant visit to Paris with his talented and beautiful wife, Petipa hardly mentions the name of his brother Lucien. Today, Lucien has been almost entirely overshadowed. When one reads the name of Petipa on an old Paris Opéra playbill, it is natural to assume that Marius is meant; but Marius never danced at the Opéra, which in his youth was the centre of the ballet universe. Lucien, the handsome elder brother, was the "successful" member of the family, the one to be emulated It was he who attained the coveted position of *premier danseur* at the Opéra (in 1839, when Marius was still a wanderer without a permanent position), who partnered Carlotta Grisi and, gossip said, won her love, who created the role of Albrecht in *Giselle*, who even had the dubious distinction of being caricatured by Honoré Daumier as *Le danseur qui se pique d'avoir conservé les belles traditions de Vestris.*

Marius was never the glamorous Paris star. He was the diligent and tireless worker, toiling unremittingly in a distant land where he still, after half a century, sometimes felt himself an exile. His memoirs leave one with the feeling that he wondered, even after he had created a company which surpassed that of the Opéra itself, whether or not he had succeeded in catching up with Lucien. Time has certainly answered that question.

Petipa was a practical man of the theatre, who considered it his duty to please the public, and he loved applause; he gloried in it. So many times, in this little book, he seems to reassure himself by repeating the phrases "great success", "dances encored", "prolonged applause". I wish that he could hear the ovations that greet Margot Fonteyn and the Royal Ballet and his choreography at the end of the Rose Adagio. Perhaps he would realize, then, that his fifty years of effort did not end in failure, after all.

THE MEMOIRS OF MARIUS PETIPA

To His Excellency
the Ober-Hofmeister
at His Imperial Majesty's Court,
the Director of the Imperial Hermitage,
IVAN ALEXANDROVICH VSEVOLOJSKY

this modest work is dedicated by a grateful
Marius Ivanovich Petipa

MARIUS PETIPA

JEAN PETIPA

MADAME LECOMTE IN "LA SYLPHIDE"
from a lithograph by H. R. Robinson

PREFACE

On May 24, 1847, I reached St Petersburg by ship, and since that time have been employed by the Imperial Theatre. Sixty years of service in one place, in one institution, is quite rare, and a destiny not granted to many mortals. Such an exceptional position gives me the courage to offer my modest memoirs to the attention of the reading public. I hope that I am not mistaken in expecting that they will interest all who are interested in the history of the Russian theatre in general, and ballet in Russia in particular.

I have had the honour of serving four Emperors: Nicholas I, Alexander II, Alexander III, and Nicholas II.

During the period of my service, the fate of the Imperial Theatre has been in the hands of five Ministers and eight Directors. The chief Ministers of the Court[1] during that time have been Prince Volkonsky, Count Vladimir Adlerberg, Count Alexander Adlerberg, Count Vorontzov-Dashkov, and Baron Vladimir Fredericks, who occupies the post at present. The Directors have been M. Gedeonov, who invited me to Petersburg, and then followed in succession: M. Saburov, Count Borch, Gedeonov (the son of the above), Baron Kister, M. Vsevolojsky, Prince Volkonsky, and finally the present Director, M. Teliakovsky. Not to seem boastful, but to show that all the predecessors of the present Director found my services useful, I would like to mention that during my service I have received the following honours:

The gold medal on the ribbon of St Stanislas, the gold medal on the ribbon of St Anne, the gold medal on the ribbon of St Vladimir, the gold medal on the ribbon of St Alexander Nevsky, the decoration of St Stanislas 3rd degree, the decoration of St Anne 2nd degree, and the decoration of St Vladimir 4th degree.

Foreign decorations: the Commander's Crosses of Roumania, Persia, and Spain; France: the Palmes Académiques and Medal for Life-Saving.[2]

NOTES TO PREFACE

(1) In Imperial Russia, the office of Minister of the Court was an important Cabinet post. The Minister who held it had charge of the entire Imperial household, including two Imperial Courts, seventeen Grand Ducal Courts, four great theatres (the Maryinsky and the Alexandrinsky in St Petersburg, the Maly and the Bolshoi in Moscow), and eleven private Court theatres.

(2) The literal translation of the title of this last decoration is "Medal for saving from drowning". Unfortunately Petipa does not describe the circumstances, nor identify the person whom he rescued.

CHAPTER I

A DANCER'S CHILDHOOD

ON March 11, 1822, in the French coastal city of Marseilles, to Jean Antoine Petipa[1] and his wife Victorine Grasseau, was born a son, Alphonse Victor Marius Petipa. That was your most obedient servant. Under the conditions of the time, I could have been considered already a servant of the stage, from my very birth. My father was a *premier danseur* and ballet master, and my mother enjoyed considerable renown as a performer of first roles in tragedies. Service to art was then transferred from generation to generation, and the history of French theatre lists many theatrical families.

The role of the city in which I saw light will be limited in my biography, because neither as an artist, nor as a man in the narrow meaning of the word, did I take any kind of steps in it. I was hardly three months old, when in June of the same 1822[2] my parents received an invitation to Brussels, whence they set out with the whole family, in a travelling coach acquired by my father for this purpose.

Today, the railroad carries travellers from Marseilles to Brussels in less than twenty-four hours, but then, for the same trip, twenty-four days was not enough. The travelling carriage became a moving apartment; in it lived our quite numerous family, and I tried to occupy the least possible place, either cuddling at the breast of my mother, who fed me, or resting on her hospitable lap. Besides us and my father in the berlin (a kind of four-wheeled carriage) there were sheltered also my brother Lucien[3] and my sister Victoria. It is not difficult for the reader to surmise that I have kept no memories of this first journey of mine, and how we reached the Belgian capital.

In Brussels I received a general education in the high
school (*gymnasium*), but paralleling this I attended the Fétis
Conservatory, where I studied solfeggio and learned to play
the violin with a comrade of mine who later became the
well-known violinist, Vieuxtemps.[4]

At seven, I started instruction in the art of dancing in the
class of my father, who broke many bows on my hands in
order to acquaint me with the mysteries of choreography.
Such pedagogical means were necessary, because in my
childhood I did not feel the smallest inclination to this branch
of art. To the young thinker, it seemed unworthy for men to
fuss before the public in all sorts of graceful poses. One way
or another, I had to overcome this great amount of knowledge, and at nine years I appeared on the stage in the ballet
La Dansomanie,[5] created by my father.

I first appeared before the public coming out of a magic
lantern, in the costume of a Savoyard, with a monkey in my
arms; my début role was that of the son of a courtier, whose
name day was celebrated in the course of the ballet.

As little as my heart was inclined towards the activities
of dancers, I gave way to the suggestions and admonitions
of my mother, whom I worshipped, and who succeeded
in convincing me that it was my duty to obey my father's
will.

My educational and theatrical occupations were interrupted for two months in preparation for my first com-
munion, which even now has great meaning in every
Catholic family, and then was considered the most sacred
religious duty of every Catholic, at the transition from
childhood to adolescence.

Upon fulfilment of this duty, I started to dance and to
play the violin again with zeal, until 1830, when a revolution
broke out in Brussels. It started during a theatrical performance, after the prayer in the well-known opera *Fenella*, or *La
Muette de Portici*.[6]

At the cry of "To arms, to arms!" the tenor, Lafeuillade,

still in the costume of Masaniello, rushed out into the street, where a huge crowd of revolutionaries were waiting for him.

The opera conspirator carried into reality the hero whom he played, and continued his role in real life, not even changing his costume; the stage exerted its influence on the crowd and gave an impetus to one of the greatest liberating movements of the first half of the nineteenth century.

For a full fifteen months, the theatres discontinued their activities. This was a bad time for my father. It was not easy to feed the family, being deprived of the main source of income; often we lacked the bare necessities, because my father had to be satisfied with the small amount received from two boarding schools where he taught social dance. My brother Lucien and I helped our father by copying music for Prince Trezine, a passionate lover of waltzes and quadrilles, which he himself composed in incredible quantity. But neither our earnings nor father's income was enough for more than a meagre existence.

Soon after the revolution started, Dutchmen were hidden in the Antwerp citadel, situated a few miles from Antwerp. The French and Belgians joined in great strength in this city, and prepared to attack the citadel.

In extreme need, and after lengthy hesitation, my father decided to rent the Antwerp theatre and take the risk, in view of the critical times, of giving a few ballet performances in this theatre, the entire company consisting only of members of his family.

We went to Antwerp. On the day following our arrival we decorated every corner and fence with posters, bringing to the attention of the public, the following:

First performance of the famous company of
M. Petipa, ballet master of the grand
Théâtre de la Monnaie, in Brussels

THE MILLERS
Ballet in Three Acts
Cast

The Miller	Petipa, father
The Miller's Wife	Petipa, mother
Lisette (*their daughter*)	Mlle. Victoria P.
Colin	Lucien P.
Gilles (*comic character*)	Marius P.

Male and female Peasants

The latter were supernumeraries hired in the city and trained by father. There were no lamps in the theatre. How to light it? Necessity is the mother of invention. Father ordered tallow candles to be put into large potatoes, which in turn were stuck directly to the floor, between the wings. These improvised candlesticks did their job, but at the end of the performance a small incident occurred, which fortunately ended all right, and amused the not very numerous public. From our rapid and energetic movements in the final *galop*, the potatoes became unglued, rolled onto the stage, and appeared suddenly at out feet. Several officers seated in the auditorium burst into jolly laughter, and rewarded us with loud applause. Returning to the hotel, after the performance, we, the younger generation, were still laughing, but our father and mother had no heart for laughter, crushed by the miserable receipts. In the cash-box there were only 60 francs, in all.

The following morning my father held a conference with my mother, deliberating on the question of whether we should risk giving a second performance. There were no special expectations of large receipts, but there was no other way out – we had to pay the hotel and coach, and had no money at all. Leaving to our parents the decision of this vital question, the young forces of the company, that is, my brother, sister, and I, went out into the street.

Suddenly a carriage rolled into the hotel driveway, and stopped for the changing of the horses. The doors of the berlin opened, and out stepped a gentleman. Seeing us, he approaches and asks, with astonishment:

"What brought you here, children?"

It was the great tragedian, Talma.[7] He knew our family, was Lucien's godfather, and therefore kissed us all tenderly. My brother tells him, in full detail, about our performance of the previous evening, not omitting to inform him of the complete absence of an audience.

We wanted to tell our father immediately, about meeting M. Talma, but he forbade this, called the *maître d'hotel*, and ordered him to bring some figs. He decided on this treat because it was found everywhere because of the fashion for a dessert called *quatre mendiants*, consisting of figs, raisins, almonds, and nuts. This was a cheap, unperishable dessert, and therefore was served in all second-class hotels and on every table d'hôte.

Ordering us to turn away, so as not to see what he was preparing to do, Talma stuck three *louis d'or* in each of the three figs which he gave us, accompanying the treat with kisses.

"Tell your father and mother that in two months I will visit them in Brussels."

He said this, seated himself in his travelling carriage, and hurried away.

Waving our handkerchiefs in farewell, we rushed into the hotel and ran up the stairs in the twinkling of an eye, to tell our father the good news. There, he sprang to the window and loudly shouted "Talma! Talma!", but the tragedian was already far away. We three, interrupting each other, choking with delight, shouted:

"Papa! Mama! Look inside the figs! In each of them are three *louis d'or*! M. Talma told us not to look, but we saw what he was doing, anyway!"

Father and mother, exchanging looks, said: "What a noble way to help us."

"*Garçon*," calls our father, "the check!" – and turns to our mother: "I will go at once to reserve places on the stage-coach which leaves at four o'clock, and you pack our things. Before our departure, we must have a good lunch."

And we all raised a sincere cry, "Long live Talma!"

On returning to Brussels, and having gone to the Place de la Monnaie, we saw that it already exhibited a Tree of Freedom, in all its beauty. On seeing this tree, my father was reminded of a couplet composed by the opera chorister Dubut, which ended in a refrain sung to the tune of *La Brabançonne*:

> Before, we were paid 100 francs,
> And now, only 30,
> But now we also have a Tree of Freedom!

Before the revolution, the choristers had been paid 100 francs a month; when the theatres reopened, the management offered them only 30 francs because of *force majeure*, and the poor people had to agree to accept, because the "freedom" of choice was not theirs.

NOTES TO CHAPTER I

(1) Jean Antoine Petipa (1787-1855) danced at the Théâtre de la Porte Saint-Martin, Paris, under Jean-Baptiste Blache, in 1815. He spent many years at the Théâtre de la Monnaie, Brussels, and made its ballet company one of the finest in Europe. Jean Petipa preceded his son, Marius, to St Petersburg, accepting a post as professor at the Imperial Academy of Dancing in 1845. He died in St Petersburg ten years later.

(2) It was in May, 1819, not 1822, that Jean Petipa took his family from Marseilles to Brussels, where on May 20 he made his début in the ballet *Almaviva et Rosine* at the Théâtre de la Monnaie (where he worked 1819-31, 1833-5, 1840-4). Marius Petipa says that he was a baby at the time of this journey, so it seems obvious that he was born in 1819, not 1822. Furthermore, the Russian authority Valérian Svetloff (in *Le Ballet Contemporain*, p. 9) confirms that Petipa's date of birth was 1819.

(3) Lucien Petipa (1816-1900) is often confused with his brother Marius. Lucien, for many years *premier danseur* and choreographer at the Paris Opéra, created the role of Albrecht in *Giselle*, partnered Carlotta Grisi, Fanny Cerrito, Carolina Rosati, Amalia Ferraris, and Emma Livry, and staged the Bacchanale for the first Paris production of Wagner's opera *Tannhäuser*. His last choreographic work was Edouard Lalo's *Namouna*, produced at the Paris Opéra in 1882, with Rita Sangalli in the title role.

(4) Henri Vieuxtemps (1820-81), one of the most distinguished violinists of his time, lived in Brussels 1831-3, between several tours he made as a musical prodigy.

(5) *La Dansomanie*, ballet by Pierre Gardel, was first produced at the Paris Opéra June 14, 1800, with Branchu, Goyon, Auguste Vestris, Marie Adelaide Duport, and Gardel himself in the cast. Jean Petipa's *La Dansomanie* was probably a restaging of this work by Gardel.

(6) Fenella, a dumb girl, is the principal female character in Daniel François Auber's opera *La Muette de Portici*, frequently called *Masaniello* after the leading tenor role. At the performance described by Petipa, which took place on August 25, 1830, Fenella was danced by Madame Benoni (née Feltmann).

(7) François-Joseph Talma (1763-1826), the most celebrated French tragedian of his time, who numbered Napoleon among the admirers of his artistry, died in Paris in 1826, four years before the Belgian revolution of 1830. Petipa, in his old age (he was over eighty when these memoirs were written), must have confused the difficult time following the Belgian revolution with some earlier period of financial difficulty, when Talma came to the assistance of the family. Marius Petipa's vivid recollection of Talma is another indication that he was born earlier than 1822.

CHAPTER II

ACROSS THE ATLANTIC AND BACK

AFTER a twelve-year stay in Belgium, my father received an invitation to occupy the position of ballet master in Bordeaux. We spent four years in this city, and there I started to study dance seriously, and to examine the theory of *pas*.

I was sixteen when I obtained my first independent engagement as first dancer and ballet master, in Nantes. Here I had only to create dances for the opera, stage one-act ballets of my own creation, and devise ballet numbers for divertissements. Besides myself, as *premier danseur*, the troupe had: second male dancer, comic, two *premières danseuses*, one second, sixteen male supernumeraries, and sixteen female supernumeraries. The body of the ballet troupe was not large, but I composed and staged with them, three ballets:

Le Droit du Seigneur
La Petite Bohémienne
La Noce à Nantes

Besides the salary I received for the ballets I created, I got a special author's fee on the scale of ten francs for each performance.

This insignificant fee strongly flattered my ego, and I decided to devote myself to this specialty.

I was happy in this position, and remained a second season, but misfortune fell upon me: on stage, dancing, I broke my shinbone, and spent six weeks in bed. There I came to know how the majority of impresarios treat the actors whom they exploit. At the end of the month, I gave my mother power of attorney to receive my salary, but although I had broken my leg during the fulfilment of my duty on stage, the director still refused to make any payment, on the basis of the conditions of my contract. What to do? How to get the second month's salary from them? I still could not use my leg, but I had to take part in the performance. I devised a new Spanish *pas*, in which with my hands I showed another dancer how to work the feet, and myself appeared, accompanying the *pas* with castanets. The management found itself legally defeated, and with a change of heart paid all my salary for the second month. But the job with these gentlemen did not appeal to me any more, and with pleasure I set out for New York, with my father. We took a sailing ship, and crossed the ocean in exactly twenty-two days.

Sad was our acquaintance with the United States, where an impresario, a certain Lecomte, had brought us promising mountains of gold, and where we soon found that we had fallen into the hands of an international adventurer.

My father was engaged as ballet master, I as *premier danseur*, and we appeared within five days of our arrival in New York. The opening took place with some kind of play and ballet; the first performance had full box office receipts, bits of which fell into our hands in the form of an insignificant advance. A week passed, the receipts were good, but they paid us only half of the salary due, and after the second week they cynically, categorically explained that there was no money and they couldn't pay us, but asked us to be patient. We waited patiently for the third and fourth weeks, but then the impertinence of the swindler-impresario passed all bounds, which circumstance, together with the danger of catching yellow fever, then raging there, obliged my father to escape from this, for us, inhospitable city.

Happily we learned that some kind of sailing ship was leaving for France, and we went on it, not even attempting to collect a thing from the adventurer. Afterwards, we learned that we had acted very sensibly, because the enterprise ended in a most shameful bankruptcy, and the company who worked the full time didn't receive a cent.[1]

Upon returning to Paris, and not having an engagement, I started to perfect myself in the class of the then famous old Vestris.[2] My brother Lucien was already dancing in the Paris Grand Opéra; I, also, wanted to appear on some Parisian stage, and the opportunity presented itself. Having worked for two months with my talented professor, I was blessed with such good luck as I hadn't dared to dream. I took part in the benefit of the great actress Rachel,[3] where I danced with such a great star as the then sensational Carlotta Grisi.

Participation in such an outstanding performance made me known, and within a few days I received an invitation to Bordeaux, in the capacity of *premier danseur*. We were five débutant artists, but the engagement of each débutant was final only after the third début, when the public, or the faithful subscribers, pronounced their judgement. With fear and trembling, each artist awaited the approach of the decisive moment.

The curtain falls and the *commissaire*, who is seated in one of the boxes, gets up. Tomblike silence.

"The tenor, Faure, is accepted by a large majority." –

Applause, hisses, and even whistles, but the protesting minority must submit to the decree of the applause. Tenor Faure is accepted.

The same procedure is repeated upon the announcement of the name of Marie Lezaire, the first soubrette in comedy; she is also acknowledged to be engaged, to the noisy accompaniment of applause, whistles, and hisses.

More dead than alive, we stood in the wings during the moment when our fates were decided; on this decision depended not only the security of the season, but our entire subsequent careers. My turn came.

"M. Marius Petipa, *premier danseur* – "

I hear "bravo, bravo!", but hisses also are heard. Who

will win? I can assure you that I shook as in a fever, and long afterwards could not forget the agony I experienced.

"Quiet, please!" shouts the *commissaire*. All became still, and I, it may be well understood, am all ears.

"M. Petipa is accepted, after three débuts, by the decision of the majority of the audience, because he had such a great and fully deserved success in *Giselle*, *La Péri*, and *La Fille mal Gardée*." Again applause, and here I am with a job. Such an examination an artist must pass even now in the provincial theatres of France, where they receive subsidies from the city and where their financial fate is in the hands of subscribers. Not a single enterprise could subsist on the support of the transient public.

Although I was not ballet master, I succeeded in staging, in the luxurious theatre of this wonderful city, four ballets which were successful and always made money.

Here are, more or less, my outstanding works:

> *La Jolie Bordelaise*
> *Les Vendanges*
> *L'Intrigue Amoureuse*
> *La Langage des Fleurs.*

NOTES TO CHAPTER II

(1) The little ballet company which brought Jean and Marius Petipa to America was headed by Mme Lecomte (née Martin), who had danced at the Paris Opera and the King's Theatre, London, and had been Jean Petipa's *première danseuse* in Brussels in 1830. She had already appeared in the United States for two seasons. In 1839 her company included, in addition to the two Petipas, her brother Jules Martin and his wife, a German eccentric dancer and mime named Kaiffer, and Mlle Pauline Desjardins, who later toured the United States with Fanny Elssler. The unpopular company manager was the ballerina's husband, G. Lecomte, a retired tenor who had also appeared, earlier, in Brussels.

The company opened at the National Theatre, New York, October 29, 1839, in Jean Coralli's ballet *La Tarentule*, staged by Jean Petipa, with Mme Lecomte as Lauretta, Jules Martin as Luigi (the *premier danseur's* role), and one of the Petipas – the programme, preserved in the Harvard Theatre Collection, does not distinguish between them – as Dr Omeopatico, a quack physician.

As Petipa recalls, the ballet season was a financial failure. By November 12 (after Jean Petipa had staged another ballet, *Jocko, the Brazilian Ape*) the American manager of the theatre, James W. Wallack, withdrew the dancers. They found another engagement at the Bowery Theatre, where they reopened on November 21, in *Jocko*. Two days later Jean Petipa produced his third ballet, *Marco Bomba, or the Bragging Sergeant*, with Marius as Nunez. (This work appeared in the repertoire of the Bolshoi Theatre, St Petersburg, in 1857, with choreography credited to Jules Perrot.) On November 23, the season closed with a pitiful attempt at a flourish, when a "Grand Carnival and Masked Ball, arranged and produced by Monsieur Petipa," was added to *Marco Bomba*. This was the last American appearance of the two Petipas.

Mme Lecomte, however, spent the winter touring all the way to the western frontier on the Mississippi river, dancing in such remote towns as St Louis, Mobile and New Orleans in a repertoire which included *La Sylphide*, *Le Dieu et la Bayadère*, and Jean Petipa's *Marco Bomba*.

For a complete account of the Petipas' visit to New York, see *Dance Index*, Volume I, No. 5 (May 1942): *The Petipa Family in Europe and America*, by Lillian Moore.

(2) Auguste Vestris (1760-1842), son of Gaetan Vestris and the ballerina Marie Allard, was one of the most brilliant dancers of his time, and later an excellent teacher. Fanny Elssler, Pauline Duvernay, and August Bournonville attended his classes. When Marius Petipa studied under him, on his return from America, Vestris was already eighty, and had but two more years to live.

(3) Elisa Félix, known as Mlle Rachel (1820-58), was a celebrated tragedienne, noted for her profoundly moving interpretations of the great dramas of Racine. Phèdre, Bérénice and Athalie were among her greatest roles.

NATIONAL THEATRE

Broadway, ... adjoining Niblo's Gardens.

Tickets and places for the Parquette and Boxes to be secured at the BOX OFFICE OF THE THEATRE, and at
DAVIS & HORN'S Music Store, No. 367 Broadway.

FIRST NIGHT OF THE BALLET PANTOMIME

LA TARANTULE,

IN WHICH

Mons. PETITPA,
Mons. MARTIN,
Mons. KAIFFER,
Madame LECOMTE,
M'lle. Pauline DESJARDIN,
Madame KLISHNIG,
Madame MARTIN,

And the CORPS DE-BALLET of the Theatre will appear.

TUESDAY EVENING, OCTOBER 29th, 1839,

Will be acted, first time this season, the Drama of the

Maid of Croissey

After which will be produced, with NEW SCENERY, DRESS S and PROPERTIES; the celebrated
BALLET PANTOMIME in 2 acts, entitled

LA TARANTULE!

Being the last novelty produced at the ACADEMIE ROYALE, PARIS. Written by Mons CORALY. The Music by MONS GIDE. The Dances arranged and the action of the piece produced under the direction of Mons PETITPA, Ballet Director from the principal Theatres of Paris, Naples, Vienna, Brussels, &c.; with the following cast:

Luidgi..........................Mons. MARTIN | M me..........................Madame KLISHNIG
Ossapalies.......................Mons. PETITPA | Clorinde........................Madame MARTIN
Lorrenzo.........................Mons. KAIFFER | Jacinta........................M'me. PAULINE DESJARDINS
Laurento.........................Madame LECOMTE

Corps-de-Ballet, and Assistants in the representation, by members of the National Company.

DANCES TO BE PERFORMED DURING THE BALLET.

ACT I.

Various PAS.................by Madame LECOMTE and the Ladies of the Corps-de-Ballet
Introduction,.....................by the Corps-de-Ballet
GRAND PAS DE DEUX....by Mons. KAIFFER and M'lle. PAULINE DESJARDINS
THE CELEBRATED TARENTELLE,.........by M'me LECOMTE & Mons. MARTIN
Grand ACTION OF PANTOMIME,........by Madame LECOMTE and FINALE to ACT

ACT II.

Grand display of Dancing and Pantomimic Action,...by M'me. LECOMTE & Mons. PETITPA
GRAND PAS SEUL by Madame LECOMTE, in which she will give a representation of the
Paroxysms of excitement and madness occasioned by the bite of the Tarentula!
A NEW GALLOPADE arranged expressly for this occasion by Mons. PETITPA will be executed by M'me. LECOMTE, M'lle. DESJARDINs, M'lle. KLISHNIG, Mons. MARTIN, Mons. KAIFFER, and the entire CORPS-DE-BALLET.

The following Scenery, painted by BENGOUGH.

Act 1. Scene 1. Village and Distant Country.
Act 2d. Scene 1. Chamber in the Post House.
Scene 2. High Road—and Distant Mountains.

To conclude with the Farce of a

GENTLEMAN IN DIFFICULTIES

Mr. Sedley..........................Mr. Browne
Mr. Crisp..........................Baker
Mr. Simmons..........................Walton
Servant..........................Barrett
Mrs. Crisp..........................Mrs. Russell
Mrs. Sedley..........................Mrs. Rogers
Mrs. Simmons..........................Mrs Plumer
Pimmay..........................Miss Ayres
Dorothy..........................Mrs. Baldock

WEDNESDAY—Will be acted Bulwer's Play of the

"LADY OF LYONS."

Claude Melnotte . . . . . . Mr. Charles Kean
His 1st appearance in that character in New-York.

Pauline . . . . Mrs. G. Barrett
Her 1st appearance at this Theatre—and 1st night of her engagement, which is for a limited period.
With a popular Farce.

THURSDAY. MR. C. KEAN IN A FAVORITE CHARACTER.

Mr. C. KEAN will act on Wednesday and Thursday.

The programme of the first appearance in New York of
Marias and Jean Petipa, 29th October, 1839.

CHAPTER III

A DUEL IN SPAIN

AFTER I had spent only eleven months in Bordeaux, the enterprise of the director of that time, Deveria, ended in disaster, but my name was already well known, and only a short time passed without a job. I was immediately invited to Madrid, to the Royal Theatre, under the jurisdiction of Salamanca,[1] the Court Minister. There I had something to be proud of. I signed for a salary of 12,000 francs, a benefit, and a two-month vacation. In that same season the famous tenor, Tamberlik,[2] was invited to the Madrid stage. We immediately became bosom friends. This friendly relationship continued afterwards in Petersburg, where work again brought us together.

I had a two-month vacation, but it was not used for rest; with the *première danseuse*, Mlle Guy-Stéphan,[3] I used it to tour all the big cities of Andalusia, where an outstanding success awaited us. Without boasting, I can say that I danced and played the castanets no worse than the first dancers of Andalusia. The warm, passionate children of happy Andalusia were carried into ecstasy, into forgetfulness of everything, until they could neither sit still nor stand in their places, when this epitome of their national dance began. Therefore, it is not hard to understand what enthusiasm was aroused in them, when a foreigner performed their national dance.

During the tour, we happened to be present at the big festival in San-Lúcar, where were gathered all the well-known *cuadrillas*, the *picadors*, and others who followed the toreadors, for the bullfights which take place in the biggest Spanish arenas.

14

All the richest, most noble Spaniards gathered there, to enjoy for three days the best-loved show in Spain. There was a bullfight every day for three days. In the evenings, all the visiting and local families fill the streets or gather on the big hotel balconies. In every street, masked students give concerts on their guitars and mandolins. As soon as they start to play the famous *fandango*, the couples form, and all is forgotten in the whirlwind of dancers.

I wore a Spanish costume, I felt just like a Spaniard, and audaciously invited an attractive Spanish woman to dance; and together with three other couples we tempestuously, madly did this characteristic Spanish dance.

I danced with passion, a worthy son of Andalusia, for one could not but be carried away by the surrounding setting: the students with guitars in place of an orchestra, their shouting, the picture illuminated by another group of students with torches in their hands. Performers, spectators – all rising to a mad excitement; people throwing money to the students, which inspired them with still more enthusiasm, and their enthusiasm infected the rest. Shouts, shrieks, laughter, cloaks thrown under the feet of the dancing girls, everyday life with its troubles forgotten – the crowd has only one cult – passion.

I will permit myself a little digression. From the above explanation it is evident that I became familiar with Spanish dances first hand, at the source. But imagine! I inserted this genuine, original *fandango* in the opera *Carmen*, on the Petersburg stage, where it had a huge success. But it happened that I fell ill, and the Director expressed the wish that this dance be replaced with another *pas* "more Spanish", and thought of something that resembled, I can assure you, a Chinese dance instead of Spanish.

They wanted at all costs to eliminate the dances I had created, but they forgot, or, if you like, they didn't understand that it was not my invention, but the national dance that I had learned when I was in Madrid.

I return there again. In my time, the marriage of the Duke de Montpensier took place; in my time also, though a bit later, the marriage of Queen Isabella. In celebration of the Queen's marriage, a gala celebration was held, and I created a one-act ballet, *Carmen and her Toreador*.

In Madrid I staged a few more of my ballets: *The Pearl of Seville*, *The Adventure of the Daughter of Madrid*, *The Flower of Granada*, and *The Departure for the Bullfight*. There, also, I created and launched a polka which went around the whole world.

In Spain, as everywhere else, there are certain indigenous customs and manners, from which an inhabitant will never permit himself to depart; but for a long time it has been well known, that forbidden fruit is the sweetest. As a foreigner I bravely, and occasionally even too bravely, allowed myself such a departure, which left me liable to persecution by the administrative powers; but such pranks placed me on a hero's pedestal, and created a big success with the public, who rewarded me with loud ovations.

I will give two examples of my "youthful heroism", and the second, as you will see, cost me quite enough.

Spain is a country of love and adoration of women, but at the same time, it has customs sharply at variance with the free, open-hearted display of passion which is characteristic of all Spanish dances. On the stage, an artist is strictly forbidden to kiss a woman, even if it is required in the course of the action.

In one of the Tyrolian character dances, which I did with Mme Guy-Stéphan, the dancer begs a kiss of his partner, but is met with a refusal. Still a second time he perseveres, begs the same – again a refusal. The third attempt of the lover softens the lady, she agrees, and I, getting into the role, take advantage of the received permission with such a realistic reproduction of the intended act, that even the worshippers of the school of Mr Stanislavsky would be filled with satisfaction. As soon as I left the stage, and withdrew

MARIE GUY-STÉPHAN

CARLOTTA GRISI AND LUCIEN PETIPA
IN "GISELLE"

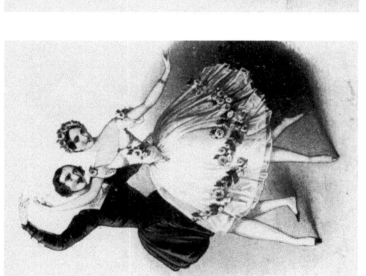

CARLOTTA GRISI AND LUCIEN PETIPA
IN "LE DIABLE À QUATRE"

to the wings, I found myself in the presence of the chief of the Madrid police, who had left his box and rushed to the stage, in order to announce to me the strictness of the prohibition of kissing a lady on the stage.

While I was meekly listening to the reprimand of His Excellency, there was a groan from the audience: the public was demanding an encore, with stormy applause and loud cries of *bis, bis!* I turn to the director, Salamanca, with a naïve air, and ask if I may repeat the number in all its dimensions – that is, is it permissible to kiss the lady again?

"Kiss as much as you like", answers the Minister.

We enter, and take our pose, to the unanimous applause of the whole house, and begin our *pas*; a tomb-like silence replaces the storm, and with strained attention everyone waits for the approach of the critical moment of kissing. The first request – refusal; the second – also; after the third – a piquant pause. She pantomimes, "Yes, you may," and two loud kisses are heard. This time I double the dose, and the excitement of the public is boundless; the whole audience, as one person, applaud my "heroic" deed, and all eyes are ironically turned towards the box of the powerful chief of police. Infuriated, he runs to the stage, and in a far from amiable tone, says to me:

"Monsieur Petipa! Trouble yourself to change clothes. I will wait for you here, and I ask you to come with me – you are under arrest!"

The Director, who is also a Court Minister, takes me under his protection, says a few reassuring phrases to the chief of police, and the business is terminated. I am rescued from the pleasure of becoming acquainted with the charming Spanish jail cells.

The second occurrence of "heroism" was in a romantic situation, and I had to show my bravery not in daring kisses, but facing the barrel of a pistol, whose owner sincerely wished, if not to kill me, in any case to seriously cripple.

An "eminent Spanish lady", no longer young but still

c

beautiful, had a subscription box at the theatre; she used to come to the theatre with her no less beautiful and quite young daughter. I don't know whether my success with the public, or my eloquent steps and *entrechats* acted on the romantic imagination of the young girl, but between us sprang up a romance according to all the rules of Spanish love affairs. After the performance, I set out to the balcony of my loved one, and if there wasn't a white handkerchief on it, which meant "danger", I climbed up on the balcony with the agility of a Spanish hidalgo, and fell into the embrace of the enchanting Juliet.

But the "eminent Spanish lady" did not always sleep soundly, and she also had her Romeo, who proved to be a compatriot of mine, the first secretary of the French Embassy, Marquis X.[4] Having learned of my noctural visits and suspecting me to be a rival, he spied on me one dark night, and, accompanied by a servant who lit his path with a torch, sprang upon me before I had time to get to the balcony. Fortunately I succeeded in avoiding a beating, and firmly clutching my stiletto, I started to admonish the Marquis, whom I recognized, that such a treacherous attack from behind was unworthy of a Frenchman, and that apparently he forgot that in a foreign country Frenchmen always meet their adversaries face to face.

"All right," he says to me, "I will await you in the morning, with my seconds, at such and such a place."

And we parted. It was after one; to whom could I turn? Who to ask to be a second? I rush to a comrade of the theatre, I ask him to do me a friendly service, but I meet a cold, categorical refusal. I remembered a tradesman from Bordeaux, who had settled in Madrid not long before. He had arrived without any money, and seeing my name on a poster, as he had seen it so recently on the posters of his home town, he came directly to me, telling me that he is a master with billiard balls, wants to occupy himself with this business in Madrid, but has not one cent for equipment. At this time I had several hundred francs, and I gave them to him without a second thought; his business got off to a good start, and I got, in him, an absolutely trustworthy friend, ready to do anything for me. Notwithstanding the late hour, I sent for him, and he did not delay in appearing.

"Here is the situation!" and I told him of my adventure.

"Command me! My life, if necessary, is at your service."

"I thank you! So you, this means, will be my second; do everything the Marquis' seconds do, and keep quiet – all the time, keep quiet."

At dawn we set out for the stipulated point; it caused him considerable difficulty to find a carriage, for they were not abundant in Madrid even in the daytime.

We drew near, and heard a shot – that was the Marquis trying his pistols, his second, the Duke d'Alba, told us.

"Permit us to do the same," says my modest witness, who was present at a duel for the first time. When I shot, he quietly observed:

"I see, with pleasure, that you shot without a miss, as before."

I was astonished at the ingenuity of this simple plebeian, who instinctively knew that to frighten my opponent, and deprive him of the necessary coolness of mind, meant to give me a better chance of a fortunate (for me) outcome of the duel.

Before starting the duel, the Duke says to me, "I am authorized by my client to offer you 10,000 francs, if you will leave Madrid immediately."

"Tell your client that I will accept the money only upon the condition that for each franc, he is given a slap in the face."

"Then to places!" shouts the Marquis, in a frenzy, "I'll show you!"

"We'll see," I reply, "who will teach whom," and we get into position. The first shot belongs to him, the gun misfires, and I propose to him to begin again.

He shoots – a miss; and my bullet shatters his lower jaw-bone.

An explanation followed: I convinced him that I don't even know the "eminent Spanish lady", and I have been visiting someone else, whose name I have no right to mention.

The story of the duel flew around the whole city, and long before my next performance the ticket office was entirely sold out; everyone wanted to see the "hero", and the ovation which I received is difficult to describe. For many more days, the appearance of my name on the poster assured the theatre of full receipts; but unfortunately I soon had to leave the city, because of the intrigues of the Embassy. I was also invited to the police station, for questioning about the duel, which was strictly prohibited, but on the advice of an agent who felt favourably towards me, I said only "no" to all the questions.

"You fought a duel?"

"No!"

"You wounded the Marquis X?"

"No!"

And with this I escaped legal prosecution, but, as I said before, I was soon obliged to leave for France.

NOTES TO CHAPTER III

(1) José, Marques de Salamanca, was the impresario of the Teatro del Circo, Madrid (the predecessor of the Teatro Real, and the fashionable home of opera and ballet in that city) from 1842 to 1850. It was at the Teatro del Circo that Petipa danced.

(2) Enrico Tamberlik (1820-89), a dramatic tenor who later became famous in such roles as Florestan in *Fidelio*, Manrico in *Il Trovatore*, and the title role in Gounod's *Faust*, first sang at the Teatro del Circo, Madrid, in 1845, during Marius Petipa's engagement there.

(3) Marie Guy-Stéphan (1818-73) had danced for two seasons in London, in such roles as Myrtha in *Giselle* and Giannina in *Ondine*, before her engagement in Madrid. There she became remarkably proficient in Spanish national dances, but was also admired for the precision and virtuosity of her classic ballet technique.

(4) The mysterious "Marquis X" was, as Ivor Guest has discovered, the Comte Lionel de Chabrillan, who later married Céleste Mogador, notorious beauty who had danced at the Bal Mabille. At the time of his death, the Comte de Chabrillan was French consul in Australia.

CHAPTER IV

MY ARRIVAL IN ST PETERSBURG

I spent some time in Paris, where I participated in the farewell benefit of Therese Elssler, who was retiring from the stage. The sisters Fanny and Therese Elssler,[1] my brother Lucien and I danced a *Pas de Quatre* on the stage of the Paris Opéra.

Soon after this, I received a letter from the old ballet master, Titus,[2] offering me an engagement in St Petersburg. I was to replace the *premier danseur*, Gredelue,[3] a very talented artist, who was leaving for Paris. The letter was quite laconic:

"M. Petipa:
His Excellency, M. Gedeonov, the Director of the Imperial Theatres, offers you the position of *premier danseur*. The salary is 10,000 francs a year and half a benefit."

I hastened to reply that I accepted.

Although the engagement offered me was very interesting, my adoring mother could not reconcile herself to the thought that her favourite would have to live in Russia, of which very little was then known, except about its strange customs and bitter cold, which were legendary.

"You wrap yourself up well," she told me over and over again, "Take care that your nose and ears don't freeze. It is so cold there, that the streets have to be heated!"

I set out for Le Havre, and on the following day got a place in a ship bound for St Petersburg. Unpacking my suitcase, I discovered three scarves, packed there by the anxious hands of my mother. She was very much disturbed about the fate of my nose, which would have to bear the

22

THE "GUITAR" CARRIAGE

A portion of a lithograph by G. Engelmann and Renoux, after a water-
colour by A. Cadolle, reproduced in *Vues de Moscou* (Paris 1825)

FANNY ELSSLER DANCING THE "PAS STRATÉGIQUE"
IN "CATARINA"

FANNY ELSSLER IN "LA SYLPHIDE"

onslaught of frosts so severe that even the bears could hardly stand them.

On shipboard I made the acquaintance of a famous actress, Mme Volnys,[4] who also had an engagement in Russia. Her aunt, a very fat and jolly woman, was travelling with her as wardrobe mistress, and we passed the time so pleasantly that we hardly noticed when Kronstadt came into view.

We arrived on May 24, 1847. We showed our passports, and were transferred to another boat which delivered us at the St Petersburg customs-house, which was then located on the Gagarin Quay. The day was hot; I took off my hat, put it on a bench, and hurried to open my suitcase and the trunks of Mme Volnys, who had asked me to help her go through the customs.

"We will not examine the belongings of artists who have been invited to Russia for the first time," the customs in-spector told me politely. I was delighted; I bowed, and was about to take off my hat, when I remembered that I had put it on the bench. But it wasn't there. Apparently it had tempted some admirer of foreign things, who was happy to seize the opportunity to acquire it, not only without paying any duty, but absolutely free.

While still on shipboard, we had asked the captain to recommend a decent hotel, and he had given us the address of the Hotel Klee, on Mikhailovsky Street. On the conclusion of the customs formalities, we went out and looked for some sort of carriage to transport us and our belongings. Carriage drivers surrounded us, offering their services, but, oh horror! What was this? It will be difficult for the present day Peterbourgeois to understand our dismay, but those who can still remember the "guitars" which then took the place of carriages will easily understand the astonishment of a foreigner, on seeing such a vehicle for the first time. Mme Volnys did not believe her eyes, and could not imagine how men and women could ride in them.

"How do you sit? How do you arrange yourself in

such a strange machine?" she asked everyone, bewildered.

One of the drivers, a very intelligent lad, understood our perplexity, and showed us how to get into his "guitar". The men sat astride, and the ladies rode side-saddle, like Amazons. We sat down, and at once understood why a certain Englishman had offered a prize of 10,000 francs to anyone who could invent a carriage more monstrously uncomfortable than those then used in the capitals of Russia.

I seated Mme Volnys in one "guitar", while the aunt and I found places in another. Sitting astride, I managed with difficulty to clasp my hands around the vast waist of my fellow-traveller, and hold her in balance. Add to this the fact that, because of the theft of my hat, I had bound a kerchief around my head, and you can easily see what a comical picture we made. The people walking along the Nevsky Prospekt held their sides from laughter, following the example of Mme Volnys, who was giggling very hard. The aunt and I did not feel at all self-conscious, so we laughed heartily, too. Such was the gay and original manner in which I entered the gates of St Petersburg, which was to prove so hospitable to me.

On the following day, I dressed in white tie and tails, and went to introduce myself to M. Gedeonov, the Director of the Imperial Theatres. I was immediately invited into the office of His Excellency, who greeted me in a very friendly manner.

"When would you like for me to make my début?"

"*Allez vous promener*," replied the Director.

"What, your Excellency? – but you were kind enough to engage me . . ."

"I know, but surely it doesn't disturb you to have four more months of freedom?"

"Four months?" I asked, fearfully.

"Nearly that."

"But indeed, Your Excellency, in these months also, one must live."

"And live well. You will be paid your full salary. And if you need money immediately, you may draw an advance."

"I would be grateful for an advance, Your Excellency."

"Is 200 roubles enough?"

"More than enough."

"Then present this paper at the office of the Imperial Theatre, and you will get 200 roubles."

I was bursting with gratitude, and on leaving the Director, gave thanks to heaven, which had sent me such good fortune. What luck! I said to myself, yes, this is simply the promised land. To receive four months' salary for doing nothing, and to obtain an immediate advance of 200 roubles – what a contrast to the administration at Nantes, where they had refused to pay me when I broke my leg while in service.

Beside myself with excitement, I shared my happiness with my mother immediately, sending her 100 roubles, which at that time amounted to 401 francs 50 centimes, on the exchange.

NOTES TO CHAPTER IV

(1) The great ballerina Fanny Elssler (1810-84) was later to dance with Marius Petipa frequently, during her brilliant engagement in Russia, from 1848 to 1851 (see Chapter VI). Her less gifted sister, Therese (1808-78), was her constant companion and partner, sharing her contracts and shining in the reflected glory of Fanny's triumphs, until 1840. Therese did not accompany her celebrated sister to America, and does not seem to have appeared on the stage after her departure.

A bitter lawsuit over a broken contract prevented Fanny Elssler's reappearance at the Paris Opéra after her return from the United States, in 1842. Therefore, the benefit performance in which Marius Petipa participated must have taken place before Elssler's American tour, although it has not been possible to establish its exact date.

(2) Antoine Titus Dauchy, known as Titus, had been trained under Deshayes and Beaupré, and made a successful début at the Paris Opéra in 1804, as Léandre in Louis Milon's ballet *Hero et Léandre*. He was long active as a choreographer in Berlin, where Fanny Elssler, in 1830, appeared in his *Spanish Divertissement* and *The Swiss Milkmaid*. He came to St Petersburg in 1832, as second ballet master, under Alexis Blache. His first production in Russia, *The Swiss Milkmaid*, was not a success, but later he established an excellent reputation with his works *Kia-Kang*, *Caesar in Egypt*, *The Virgin Island*, and his reproductions of *La Sylphide* and *Giselle*.

(3) Emile Gredelue had been *premier danseur* in Bordeaux, under Jean Petipa, in 1835-6. Marie Taglioni may have had something to do with his engagement in Russia, for he made his first appearance there in support of her at her own St Petersburg début, in *La Sylphide*, September 6, 1837. He seems to have been better as a partner than as a soloist (a quality which the ballerina probably appreciated). After ten years in Russia, Gredelue returned to France, but apparently he was an indefatigable wanderer, for in 1852, he was dancing in Leon Espinosa's company in St Louis, Missouri, and four years later he travelled with Espinosa to California. In 1865-6 he was back in Paris, appearing in Arthur Saint-Léon's ballets at the Théâtre Italien.

(4) Madame Volnys, née Leontine Fay (1810-76) had been a popular child prodigy before achieving distinction as a comedienne of genuine taste and finesse. She made her début at the age of seven, at Namur, but won her first notable success at the Théâtre du Gymnase, Paris, when she was ten. In 1832 she married the actor Claude François Charles Joly, called Volnys, with whom she appeared at the Théâtre Français. Her husband did not accompany her to Russia, where she enjoyed great triumphs and remained for many years. She finally returned to France in 1873, and rejoined her husband in Nice, where she died three years later.

ELENA ANDREYANOVA
at La Scala, Milan   a caricature by an anonymous artist

ELENA ANDREYANOVA AND EMILE GREDELU

YRCA MATTHIAS

CHAPTER V

AN INSULT TO ANDREYANOVA

DURING the first four months of my stay in St Petersburg I became acquainted with the city. I often visited the Hermitage, and enjoyed going to the islands, but every morning I practised the art of dancing, in the school of the Imperial Theatre.

Three weeks before the opening of the season, at the Director's request, I started staging the ballet *Paquita*,[1] in which I was to make my début. I was to appear with Mlle Andreyanova,[2] who enjoyed the special patronage of His Excellency.

This artist was already far past her first youth, and did not enjoy particular favour with the public, although she was very talented and yielded nothing, in "school", to the famous Taglioni. At this time the aged ballet master, Titus, left the service of the St Petersburg Theatre, and returned to Paris for good.

The first performance of *Paquita* came and, oh happiness! I had the good fortune and honour of appearing in the presence of His Majesty the Emperor Nicholas I, who attended my début. A week later, His Majesty presented me with a ring set with rubies and eighteen marquise diamonds. There is no need to say how happy this first Royal gift made me. I have kept it until today, as a most comforting remembrance of the beginning of my career.

During that season I appeared several more times in *Paquita*, in *Giselle*, also with Andreyanova, and in *La Péri*, with Mlle Smirnova, née Vakhovitch.

My father had also been invited to St Petersburg, in the

capacity of professor of dancing for the men's classes in the school of the Imperial Theatre.

Toward the end of the season I was given a benefit, and on this occasion I appeared in a new ballet, *Le Diable Amoureux* (*Satanella*), in which Andreyanova again danced the leading role. My father also appeared in this ballet, playing the role of my tutor, with great success.

The next year I was sent to Moscow, where I was to stage the ballets *Paquita* and *Satanella*. There a very sad surprise awaited us. Dozens of subscribers from St Petersburg had followed us to Moscow, and attended the first performance of *Paquita* in the ancient capital of Russia, only to see a dead black cat thrown onto the stage, with a little card tied onto its tail, bearing the inscription:

"To the *première danseuse étoile*"

When this happened, Andreyanova was dancing with Montessu, who carried her into the wings, unconscious. This rude and tactless insult, hurled at a very capable artist, naturally infuriated the public. They sided with Andreyanova. She was called out innumerable times, and greeted with enthusiastic applause. The ovation did not calm down for a long time.[3] Three weeks later, at her benefit in the ballet *Satanella*, the public literally overwhelmed her with flowers and valuable gifts.

The second performance of this ballet was designated as my benefit. I went to Andreyanova and asked the honour of her participation.

"I will play my role with great pleasure," she replied, "but I must ask you to omit our *Pas de Deux*, because I am a little tired."

"Pardon me, Mlle Andreyanova, but I can't avoid participating in my own benefit, can I? To omit it is impossible."

"Then dance it with some other dancer."

"You will permit it?"

"Of course. Please do, M. Petipa!" she replied.

Dancing in Moscow at this time there was a beautiful young girl, Yrca Matthias,[4] who was idolized by the public. I immediately asked her to participate in my benefit, and dance the *Pas de Deux* with me, and she accepted with great pleasure.

The performance arrived, and the theatre was so crowded that an apple could not have fallen anywhere; all the admirers and worshippers of Yrca Matthias (which included everyone who attended the ballet) hurried to the theatre.

The orchestra begins the sixteen bars preceding our entrance; a rain of flowers and bouquets falls from the boxes, covering the whole stage. The orchestra stops playing, and waits until the flowers can be cleared from the stage. The conductor once more raises his baton, the orchestra starts to play, and again the stage is covered with flowers. The same involuntary entr'acte; the orchestra begins a third time, and we finally succeed in dancing the adagio, finishing under a new rain of bouquets. After the variation, there is a storm of applause, and at the conclusion of the dance, a mass of garlands, and Yrca Matthias is called out for interminable bows.

Note, that this ovation was for my partner, and although it was my benefit, only a small proportion of the applause was for me. It would seem that I might have felt rather badly, but the performance ended with an added and completely unexpected unpleasantness, which clearly illustrated the backstage manners of the star. At the end of the ballet, I went to bid Mlle Andreyanova good night, as I used to do after every performance, simply out of courtesy.

I entered, and uttered the usual greetings, but was not honoured with a reply. The Petersburg star was storming in a rage; and because of the success of another ballerina, she became my worst enemy.

NOTES TO CHAPTER V

(1) *Paquita*, a ballet by Joseph Mazilier, had been produced at the Paris Opéra on April 1, 1846, and Petipa's staging of the work in St Petersburg followed the original choreography.

(2) Elena Andreyanova (1819-57) was actually only twenty-eight years old when Petipa arrived in St Petersburg. She had been the first ballerina to dance *Giselle* in Russia, in 1842. In 1845 she appeared successfully at the Paris Opéra, and in 1846 danced briefly in Milan. She died in Paris, and is buried in the cemetery of Père-Lachaise.

(3) A letter from Marius Petipa to Gedeonov, dated at Moscow, December 6, 1848, and describing in detail the incident of Mlle Andreyanova and the dead cat, was published in *Les Archives Internationales de la Danse*, 15 juillet 1934, p. 106. According to an explanatory note accompanying the letter, the demonstration against Andreyanova was instigated by the son of the postal director, Boulgakoff, who was an admirer of Yrca Matthias. To punish him for his part in the affair, the Emperor Nicholas I exiled Boulgakoff to the Caucasus for several years.

Anatole Chujoy, in his excellent monograph *Russian Balletomania*, published in *Dance Index*, Vol. VII, no. 3, gives further details about the incident. It seems that the Moscow balletomanes resented the presence of Andreyanova not only because of their admiration for Mlle Matthias, but because she had deprived their favourite Russian dancer, Mlle Sankovska, of her best roles. After the insult to Andreyanova, Gedeonov went so far as to order that no ballet performance could be given without her participation, and to protect her against further unpleasantness, he stationed plain-clothes policemen in the front row at every performance.

(4) Yrca Matthias, born in Lyon, France, December 4, 1829, was a pupil of Joseph Mazilier. She had made her Moscow début on September 17, 1847, before her eighteenth birthday. Later she joined the Ravel troupe of dancers and pantomimists, with whom she made frequent appearances in the United States, from 1853 to 1858, in such roles as *Paquita*, *Giselle*, and *Paquerette*. She married François Ravel.

CHAPTER VI

FANNY ELSSLER AND THE EMPEROR

WHILE I was in Moscow, Fanny Elssler was invited to St
Petersburg, and started to rehearse the ballet *Esmeralda*, in
which she had created the leading role, when it had been
produced shortly before in London.[1] On my return from
Moscow, I immediately commenced the staging of this ballet.
I had finished the first act when Jules Perrot, the author of
the ballet, arrived and himself took over the production of
his wonderful work.

Afterwards, I always adhered to the recommendations and
traditions of the author, neither permitting myself the
smallest deviation, nor interpolating such disgusting tricks
as the breaking of Quasimodo's jaw during the already
heart-rending scene with Esmeralda's mother, which for
some reason was permitted on the Moscow stage.

Here is the cast of the first performance of *Esmeralda* in
St Petersburg:

ESMERALDA	Fanny Elssler
GRINGOIRE	Jules Perrot
PHOEBUS	Marius Petipa
QUASIMODO	Didier
CLAUDE FROLLO	Goltz
FLEUR DE LYS	Mlle Smirnova
MOTHER	Mlle Amosova

Every balletomane knows what a success this ballet enjoyed; and how could it be otherwise, when the principal
role was played by such a great artist as Fanny Elssler? She
was positively inimitable in this role, and all the Esmeraldas
I saw afterwards seemed pallid copies.

For a benefit performance, I created a new ballet of my own, *The Swiss Milkmaid*,[2] which met with success due to the participation of Fanny Elssler. She also appeared in *Giselle*, *Catarina*, *Le Délire d'un Peintre*, and many other ballets.

For her farewell benefit, Fanny Elssler danced *Catarina*. This performance was a magnificent triumph for the great dancer: endless ovations, flowers, expensive presents, in short, everything which the adoring public then gave to famous artists was bestowed on this beloved guest.

The ballet *Catarina* reminds me of an incident which made quite a stir at the time, when the Emperor Nicholas Pavlovich attended one of the rehearsals. The ballet master Perrot had staged this ballet in 1840.[3] Having sprained his foot, he asked me to rehearse the great *Pas Stratégique*, danced with rifles, and especially invented by him. We were rehearsing on the stage of the Bolshoi Theatre. During one of the rehearsals with Fanny Elssler and the corps de ballet, we had already reached the end of this *pas* when we were informed that His Imperial Majesty was in the theatre, and that he wished to see the rehearsal.

Appearing on the stage, His Majesty came right to me, and asked:

"What are you rehearsing, Petipa?"

"The dance with rifles, for the new ballet, *Catarina*, Your Majesty."

"Continue! I will watch too, Petipa!"

We began to rehearse again, but were immediately interrupted by the voice of His Majesty, speaking to the dancers:

"You are holding your rifles incorrectly, Mesdames! I will show you how the rifles should be handled."

Fanny Elssler and the *coryphées* came forward, in order to see better, and to master the correct military etiquette. His Majesty directed, showing how one must follow the commands "At ease!" and "Present arms!"

Elssler and all the dancers bowed low.

FANNY ELSSLER
IN "THE SWISS MILKMAID"

FANNY ELSSLER IN "LA TARENTULE"

FANNY ELSSLER IN "DANSE COSAQUE"
A lithograph by P. S. Duval after A. Newsam

"Come closer," His Majesty told Fanny Elssler, "and do everything that I do with the rifle."

She came to his side, attentively watching all of His Majesty's movements, and reproducing them exactly. The Emperor was very pleased, expressed his satisfaction, and asked when the first performance would take place.

"In eight days, Your Majesty."

"Good! I will come and applaud you."

Rumours about how His Majesty had personally showed Fanny Elssler how to handle a rifle flew through the whole city, and at the first performance this *pas* had an exceptional success, and they were obliged to repeat it several times. The star received a lavish gift from His Majesty.

This reminds me, by the way, of an incident concerning an artist of the Mikhailovsky Theatre, Vernet,[4] who played a very clever trick in order to assure himself of the honour of His Majesty's presence at his benefit. Vernet knew that almost every day the Emperor Nicholas Pavlovich took a walk from the Winter Palace to the Potzelooyev Bridge, along the Nevsky and Bolshaia Morskaia, and the public was strictly prohibited from petitioning His Majesty at this time, or making verbal requests. On the day of his benefit, Vernet also went for a walk, and waited for the arrival of His Majesty. Just as the Emperor appeared, Vernet came up beside him, took off his hat and, with head bared, bowed very low. His Majesty recognized him, stopped, and asked:

"Your benefit is today, Vernet?"

"Yes, Your Majesty!"

"Are you doing something interesting?"

"A very entertaining play, Your Majesty!"

"Good, I will come!" said the Emperor, and continued his walk.

The police immediately seized Vernet, and took him into custody. That was just what he wanted, so he followed them without complaint, and, secretly laughing at his terrible persecutors, remained under arrest.

D

Evening came, the public began to gather in the theatre, all the artists were ready, but the star of the benefit could not be found. The regisseur, Pessar, worried and anxious, did not know what to think. The Minister of the Court, the aged Prince Volkonsky, came back stage himself, to inform them of the arrival of His Majesty. The regisseur was telling the Minister about the incomprehensible absence of the star, when he was handed a note, with the following laconic contents:

"Dear friend!
I have been arrested. Free me!
Vernet."

"How, arrested?" asked the Minister, "For what? What has he done?"

"I don't know, Your Grace."

"Give me some paper. Deliver this immediately to the office of the Chief of Police. I demand that he be brought here immediately."

Of course, they freed Vernet at once. He dashed to the theatre and rushed to his dressing room, to dress for the performance. Nevertheless, it began somewhat late, and the Minister reported the circumstances to His Majesty, who was very much astonished at Vernet's arrest. After the first act, His Majesty went back stage and ordered that Vernet be summoned. The star presented himself, and with a sad face, bowed very deeply.

"What happened to you, Vernet? Why were you arrested?"

"Because, Your Majesty, you graciously started to talk to me."

"Poor Vernet! What can I do to compensate for this?"

"You will show me great kindness, Your Majesty, if you do not honour me by speaking to me on the street."

The Czar laughed heartily, and on the following day Vernet received a lavish gift – an expensive diamond ring. That was just what the sly fellow was after.

NOTES TO CHAPTER VI
(1) It was Carlotta Grisi who actually created the role of Esmeralda when Perrot's ballet was first presented at Her Majesty's Theatre, London, on March 9, 1844. Fanny Elssler did, however, take over the part later in the same season, and gave it her own distinctive interpretation. A vivid account of the original production of *Esmeralda* is to be found in Ivor Guest's *The Romantic Ballet in England*, p. 101-8.

(2) *The Swiss Milkmaid* was by no means a new theme for a ballet, although Petipa seems to have created original choreography for his version. Titus had staged a ballet of this title at the Théâtre de la Porte Saint-Martin, Paris, in 1823, and a similar work had been given in Vienna in 1826. *Nathalie, la Laitière Suisse*, staged by Philippe Taglioni, had been familiar in Paris since 1832, and Titus had, of course, produced *The Swiss Milkmaid* in both Berlin (with Elssler) and St Petersburg.

(3) Petipa is mistaken about the date of Perrot's *Catarina*, which was first produced at Her Majesty's Theatre, London, March 3, 1846, with Lucile Grahn in the title role. Elssler had danced the part with outstanding success in Italy, prior to her engagement in Russia.

(4) Victor Jacques Vernet (*c.* 1808-86) made his début at the Théâtre des Nouveautés, Paris, in 1827. He went to Russia soon after, and acted there for forty years, returning to France about 1871. He died in Nice.

CHAPTER VII

BERLIN AND PARIS

I PARTICIPATED in the repertoire mentioned above, from 1848 to 1854, when I married Marie Surovschikova, a very graceful dancer, whose figure equalled that of Venus.[1] For her I created and staged the following ballets:

> The Parisian Market (Le Marché des Innocents)
> The Blue Dahlia
> A Wedding in the Time of the Regency
> The Travelling Dancer
> The Beauty of Lebanon
> Florida

and many others.

The Director, M. Gedeonov, gave us a three months' leave, and we went abroad, stopping en route in Riga, where we gave eight performances to sold-out houses. The trip did not begin badly; we had an enormous success and large box office receipts.

Next we arrived in Berlin. I knew by hearsay that it was difficult for any ballerina to appear on the Berlin stage, where the ballet master was the father of the famous dancer Taglioni.[2] He would not admit any young artist within a cannon shot of the Royal Theatre, where his no longer young daughter had long ruled, dancing the principal roles in all the ballets created and staged by old Taglioni. Such an attitude is not peculiar to any one theatre, and on the St Petersburg stage, too, such things happen quite often.

Nevertheless, we decided to try our luck, and my wife and I went to see the Court Minister, who received us more than

LEONTINE FAY VOLNYS   LAURE MILLA

MARIE PETIPA
at the time of her appearances in Paris

MARIE PETIPA AND FELIX KSCHESSINSKI
IN THE MAZURKA IN "LA DIABLE À QUATRE"

amiably. I asked him to permit my wife to give a few performances on the stage of the Royal Theatre.

"I would be delighted, M. Petipa; we would all like to grant your request, but our ballet master, M. Taglioni, does not let anyone dance except his daughter."

Then I took a letter out of my pocket, and handed it to the Minister. It was a letter which had been given me by His Highness Prince Oldenburg, who had ordered it to be presented, through the Court Minister, to King Wilhelm.

"Well, this is a different matter," the Minister told us, skimming the letter, "Under these circumstances, your wife will be able to dance on our stage."

We left our address with the Minister, and on the following morning we were honoured by a visit from the Director of the Royal Theatre, Hultzen, who had received orders to inform us that my wife would be permitted to give six performances of the ballet, *The Parisian Market*. From the first performance to the fifth, the enthusiasm of the public increased, and after the last, the whole audience shouted: "Stay! Stay longer!"

King Wilhelm himself came back stage and told us graciously:

"I congratulate you on your enormous success. Will you give another six performances in Berlin?"

"I would be honoured, Your Majesty."

"Good! I will issue the order, and will have the pleasure of seeing you again."

After the sixth of the second series of performances, the public, overwhelmed with excitement over my wife's talent, literally covered her with flowers, and His Majesty the King sent her a splendid diamond bracelet. For staging the ballet *The Parisian Market*, I too was honoured with a gift from King Wilhelm: a gold snuff-box set with diamonds. I do not know how to say it in Russian, so I will give the phrase I used in French:

"Je ne prise pas, mais j'accepte avec joie et bonheur cette bonne prise."

After the unavoidable farewells, we set out again, and in three days were in Paris.

Once again we dress in our best, and go to the Court Minister, the Duc de Morny, who honours us by receiving us immediately. Again, the same request as in Berlin. I ask the Duke to permit my wife a few performances at the Paris Opéra. The Duchesse de Morny enters and the Duke presents us to his wife, a compatriot of my own wife, saying:

"This is a countrywoman of yours, my dear, who has come to ask your protection. She would like to dance on the stage of our Opéra."

"What do you intend to dance?" inquires the Duchess.

"A one-act ballet, Duchess: *The Parisian Market*, which I danced many times in Berlin."

"Good! I like that name, and I will do everything in my power to get His Majesty the Emperor Napoleon III to agree to be present at one of your performances at the Opéra."

And here, too, luck smiled on us – fate was pleased to have the wife of Morny a Russian, who was willing to help a compatriot, and had great influence at Court. Thanks to her patronage we received a note from the Director of the Opéra, informing my wife that she could make her début in eight days, and that she would be permitted to give six performances of the ballet *The Parisian Market* (*Le Marché des Innocents*).

The Emperor Napoleon III, the Empress Eugénie, the Duc and Duchesse de Morny and the entire court attended the first performance. My wife's grace and talent captivated everyone, and following the example of Their Majesties, the public gave her an enthusiastic ovation and innumerable curtain calls. Because of this enormous success, the Director came to ask what honorarium my wife wished to receive for her performances.

Taking advantage of the situation, and encouraged by her

success, my wife boldly told him that she did not want any
fee, but preferred to be given a benefit performance instead.

"This is more than difficult, Madame!" replied M. Royer.
"Benefits are only given for old and celebrated artists, and
then only when they are retiring from the stage."

"Is it impossible to make one exception from the usual
rule, M. *le Directeur*? I would be very grateful if you could
grant my request. This benefit would have an enormous
importance for my entire career. Indeed, world fame is
acquired only in Paris, and a benefit at the Paris Opéra would
influence my entire artistic future."

Two days later, the Director came to see us in person, and
informed my wife that the Minister had permitted him to
grant her wish. In order to avoid dancing in the same ballet,
we decided to stage *Le Diable à Quatre* for her benefit.

I had with me the orchestration of a *pas* created by the
ballet master Perrot for the St Petersburg production of his
ballet *Gazelda*. I was on a very friendly footing with Perrot,
and certainly did not think that he would object to the performance of this *pas* by my wife, in Paris. I went to see him,
and asked him to permit my wife to dance his *pas* at her
benefit.

"No, my friend, I cannot consent!"

Such an answer disconcerted me. "How? Why?"

"Because the Director here, and all the others too, have
not been at all kind to me."

"But, indeed, it is not the Director who is asking this, but
a friend of yours."

"It's all the same. I will not permit it; no, no, and no!"

"As you wish, my friend, but my wife will dance the *pas*
all the same, in spite of your prohibition. Good-bye!"

I would only have had to alter the name of the dance, and
make a few changes in it, for the work to lose all similarity
to Perrot's *pas*, so that my wife could dance it at her benefit.
But from the very beginning of my career until the last days,
I honestly gave credit to the works of others, and never

appropriated the creations of other ballet masters, as is now
freely practised in St Petersburg and Moscow, with my
works. I considered it my duty to announce on the poster:
"Mme Petipa's dance created by Perrot."

Two days later, the poster appeared. This performance
was so outstanding that I consider it interesting to give the
bill in its entirety:

"Théâtre Impériale de l'Opéra
for the benefit and farewell performance of
MME MARIE PETIPA
with the assistance of M. Tamberlik
and artists of the Opéra and the Théâtre du Gymnase.
The performance will include:
Scene III and duet, from the opera
OTHELLO, music by Rossini.
Mme Viardot, M. Tamberlik.
Trio from the opera
GUILLAUME TELL, music by Rossini.
Mme Tamberlik, Belval, Cazaux.
Le MARCHÉ DES INNOCENTS
Ballet-pantomime in one act, created by Marius Petipa,
music by Pugni.
The role of Glorietta by Mme Marie Petipa.
The new Pas, 'LA COSMOPOLITE'
created by Jules Perrot,
danced by Mme Marie Petipa.
Act IV of the opera LES HUGUENOTS
music by Meyerbeer.
Mme Marie Saxe and M. Michot
appearing for the first time in the roles of Valentine and Raoul.

THE COMING OF SPRING
Comédie-Vaudeville in one act, created by Dumanoir and Clairville.
Mme Geoffroy, Dieudonné, Victorien Ulric, and Mme Chéri-Leseuer.

DIVERTISSEMENT
1. A new Pas de Deux, created by Marius Petipa, and danced by Mme
   Marie Petipa and M. Chapuis.
2. A new Pas, danced by Mlle Zina and M. Merante.
3. A new Pas, 'Les Niniviennes', from the opera *Semiramide*, music by
   Rossini, danced by Mlles Parent, Baratte, Lamy, Leger,
   Poinet, Beaugrand and corps de ballet.
4. Mazurka, danced by Marie Petipa and M. Felix Kschessinski."[3]

We put up the poster, and two days before the performance Perrot's lawyer came to see the Director and told him that he would have to get an injunction against the performance, if Perrot's work was not taken off the programme.

"It is already too late," the Director replied. "It is impossible to change the announcements."

"In that case, I will take it to court."

"Very well! I will notify our lawyer immediately," said M. Royer.

The lawyer of the Opéra was the famous Chaix d'Est-Ange. The two lawyers stood before the judge's bench not more than two hours, while the matter was examined. The judge's decision was announced:

"M. Petipa is sentenced to a fine of five francs for the wilful announcement of Perrot's work on the poster, without the consent of the author; but in view of the fact that the performance of this *pas* has already been publicized, and that it is announced for one performance only, it may be performed at the benefit of the artist, Mme Marie Petipa."[4]

On the day after the benefit, Fiorentino, a well-known journalist and contributor to many newspapers, wrote: "There is an old saying: '... silly as a dancer.' M. Petipa has proved this to be wrong, having succeeded in getting tremendous publicity for his wife's benefit in all the papers, without spending one sou."

This benefit brought us receipts of 18,000 francs. My wife received an ovation, during which bouquets and wreaths were presented to her. This is very rarely done in the large Paris theatres.

A week later, Mlle Muravieva danced *Giselle* on this same stage.[5] She had been invited to Paris for a few performances, and she, too, had a colossal success. We purposely stayed several more days in Paris in order to be present at Mlle Muravieva's début.

NOTES TO CHAPTER VII

(1) Marie Sergeevna Surovschikova (1836-82) graduated from the Imperial Ballet School in 1854. Svelte and slender, with slim ankles and arrow-like *pointes*, she had little in common with the typical buxom, sturdy ballerina of the 1860's. She had an extraordinary flair for mime and *demi-caractère* dancing, which enabled her to shine in a wide variety of roles in spite of the fragility which prevented her from mastering spectacular *tours de force*.

(2) Paul Taglioni (1808-88), brother of the great Marie Taglioni who created *La Sylphide*, had been choreographer of the Berlin Royal Opera for about twenty-five years. The "no longer young" daughter to whom Petipa refers so caustically was also named Marie. Born in 1830, she was thirty-one, and only six years older than Marie Petipa, when Marius and his wife arrived in Berlin. This second Marie Taglioni, so often confused with her celebrated aunt, retired in 1866 to marry Prince Windischgraetz.

(3) Felix Kschessinski, brilliant character dancer and father of the ballerina Mathilda Kschessinska, had come to Paris expressly for the purpose of dancing this Polish Mazurka with Marie Petipa. Fiery and exhilarating, the dance aroused such enthusiasm that it had to be repeated at almost every performance.

(4) A more detailed account of this lawsuit is to be found in Ivor Guest's *The Ballet of the Second Empire, 1858-1870*, p. 48-49. This case, *Perrot v. Petipa*, was probably the first lawsuit over choreographic plagiarism, a time-honoured practice which had previously been rather generally accepted. Petipa's memory of the suit seems to have been somewhat confused, for actually Perrot was awarded 300 francs damages, a year after the event.

(5) Again Petipa's eighty-six-year-old memory must be blamed, not only for placing Muravieva's début a week after Marie Petipa's benefit, but for compressing Mme Petipa's two engagements at the Paris Opéra into one. Here, again, Ivor Guest straightens out Petipa's tangled dates (*op. cit.*, p. 46-49, 54-55, 59-60).

Marie Petipa made her début at the Paris Opéra on May 29, 1861. She danced *Le Diable à Quatre* during her second engage-

ment, in the summer of 1862, making her last Paris appearance
on August 9. Apparently, however, Marius Petipa and his wife
were again in Paris in the spring of 1863, when Martha Muravieva
made her début in *Giselle*, on May 8. The anecdote Petipa relates
in the next chapter, concerning the French actress Laure Milla,
belongs to a still later year.

CHAPTER VIII

A GAME OF CHESS

WE returned to St Petersburg during the sixth week of Lent. Upon our arrival, we set out to thank the Director, M. Gedeonov, for granting us a leave of absence.

"Delighted, M. Petipa, but you have returned at the right time."

"How is that, Your Excellency?"

"Next Sunday is to be the benefit of the orchestra conductor at the French Theatre, M. Josse. He has asked Mlle Milla[1] to take part in this performance, and I would like for you to create some sort of tableau vivant for her and yourself."

"With pleasure, Your Excellency."

"What kind of scene do you think you will stage?"

"I will stage *Medora and the Corsair*, Your Excellency."

"Excellent!"

Josse's benefit attracted crowds of students, ardent admirers of the beauty of Mlle Milla, to whom they intended to give an ovation. The Director of the Imperial Theatres was in his box, right next to the stage.

Our turn came. After the first tableau, the curtain opened to loud applause; it rose a second time, and we were already standing in a different pose, slightly suggestive. The public, and especially the students, became wildly excited. Their enthusiasm knew no bounds, and they gave Mlle Milla a stormy ovation.

Jealous as a youngster, Gedeonov rushed to the stage, ran to the wings, and shouted at me:

"Petipa! Such scenes may not be shown on the stage of the Imperial Theatre. I forbid it. Do you hear, Petipa? I forbid it!"

CAROLINA ROSATI
IN "LE CORSAIR"

Below, left :

MARTHA MURAVIEVA

Below, right :

EKATERINA VAZEM

MARIUS PETIPA

IN "FAUST"   IN "THE DAUGHTER OF PHARAOH"

MARIUS PETIPA IN MIDDLE AGE

"Don't listen to him," Milla whispered to me, "He is jealous of the students. We are a success, and that is all that matters. For the third pose, let's do something a little more daring."

"But the Director will be furious, and may never forgive me!"

"Don't worry. I will take the responsibility myself," she insisted.

At the sight of our final pose, there rose in the theatre a roar of shouts and applause, and the students, especially, went wild. Again the Director lost his temper, flew to the stage, and shouted at me:

"Petipa! I told you that such scenes are not to be shown on the Imperial stage! I will no longer keep you in our service, do you hear?"

We were called out on stage, and for a long, long time were greeted with shouts and applause. After the performance, Mlle Milla invited me to supper, along with the star of the benefit, and everyone who had participated.

"And will M. Gedeonov be there too?" I asked.

"Of course!"

"In that case, thank you very much! It will not give me much pleasure to listen to his remonstrances in the presence of all the artists."

"Don't be afraid! I guarantee that nothing like that will happen."

"All right, I will come!"

Half an hour later, we were all at Mlle Milla's. I crowded myself into a corner, to avoid meeting the eyes of His Excellency right away.

The Director arrived, congratulated the star, and found me immediately, in spite of my attempt to hide.

"Petipa! How could you permit such things – "

But the hostess hurried to him with a very sweet smile, and took his arm, saying: "You are my guest now, Your Excellency!"

"Yes, you are right," he sighed.

Mlle Milla came up and asked if I played chess.

"Fairly well," I replied.

"So much the better! The Director would like to play a game before supper."

"You want to make things worse! You had better find him another partner."

Paying no attention to my words, she said to the Director:

"Your Excellency, would you like to play chess until supper?"

"With whom, my dear?"

"With M. Petipa."

"With Petipa? Well, I'll try. Have the set brought out."

We sit down and begin to play, and I try to make the most stupid moves, in order to let him win, and change his wrath to mercy. After six moves, he announces "Mate!" and stands up, celebrating his victory.

"Gentlemen! Milla! Come here! I have beaten Petipa disgracefully. Now he has been punished. I don't need anything more."

Gedeonov was an extremely kind man, but affected an air of severity; we nicknamed him the "grumbler-benefactor". He was always angry, complaining, scolding, but was really very kind in his relations with all the artists.

I will give one more characteristic example. A week after Josse's benefit, my wife and I went to the Alexandrinsky Theatre, for the first performance of a new four-act play. There we witnessed a scandalous incident, unheard-of in the theatre.

A bit player, Vasiliev, was doing the role of the servant of a countess, to whom he brings a letter on a tray. He appeared on the stage staggering violently from one side to the other, dropped the tray, fell at the countess's feet, and began to vomit. A scandalous uproar, and the curtain is lowered!

The following day Vasiliev, with fear and trembling,

went to ask forgiveness of the Director. He crept unobserved into the anteroom where the Director's secretary, Prym, was seated. Seeing him, Prym cried:

"How do you dare to appear here?"

"Allow me to see His Excellency."

"Don't even think of it. Impossible!"

Hearing Gedeonov cough, the actor slipped into the office, sneaked up to the desk like a cat, and suddenly appeared at his full height in front of the Director, who was seated there.

His Excellency shouted: "Disgusting creature! Good-for-nothing! Get out of here!"

"Forgive me, Your Excellency! I won't do it any more."

"Good-for-nothing! You have told me this a hundred times, and I have forgiven you, but last night's scandal I will not forgive. You will never see your pension! Get out of here!"

At the Director's final words, Vasiliev drew two huge old pistols from the pockets of his frock coat. At the sight of the weapons Gedeonov, horrified, jumped up and started to call for help:

"Prym! Come here! Come quickly! Help! They want to kill me!"

"Don't be afraid, Your Excellency," said Vasiliev tearfully, "I don't want to kill you. Please, I beg you, buy these pistols from me, so that I can get something to feed my children. The property man could use them."

"How you frightened me, you scoundrel! Prym! Have the authorization for his pension prepared, so that I will hear no more about him."

The actor is saved; he falls at the feet of His Excellency, and, quite consoled, leaves the office.

But not for long were the artists to enjoy the kindness of the grumbler-benefactor. Four months after this incident occurred, he retired and went to Paris, where he died not long afterwards.

NOTE TO CHAPTER VIII

(1) Laure Dordet, known professionally as Mlle Milla, was a Parisian soubrette and operetta star who had won success in *Fan-Fan la Tulipe* at the Ambigu-Comique, in 1861. At the Théâtre de la Porte Saint-Martin, in 1865, she played the role of Helen of Troy in *La Lanterne Magique*. In 1867, she joined a touring troupe headed by Raphaël Felix, brother of the great tragedienne Rachel, and it was with his company that she appeared in Russia.

CHAPTER IX

THE DAUGHTER OF PHARAOH

APPOINTED as Director of the Imperial Theatres, to replace Gedeonov, was Saburov, who did not know his business at all, and fulfilled his obligations very carelessly. Among others, he invited to our ballet Mlle Rosati,[1] a dancer far from her first youth. She made her début in the ballet *Jovita*, and had no success at all.

With the appointment of Saburov, my position changed, too. Shortly after the production of the ballet *Jovita* our ballet master, Perrot, went to see the Director to discuss the renewal of his contract.

Entering the office of His Excellency, Perrot addressed him in the following words: "I have the honour of presenting myself to *M. l'Impresario* . . ."

"M. Perrot!" the Director interrupted, "You ought to know that I am not an impresario, but a dignitary of His Majesty . . ."

"Your Excellency," replied Perrot, "The Director of a theatre is also called an impresario."

"No, M. Perrot! For the second time I must tell you that I am an important dignitary in the service of the State!"

So saying, he turned and went out, leaving Perrot alone. The latter waited for a while, muttered: "And certainly a fool, too!" and left. A few days later he left for France, forever.

The post of ballet master was offered to me, and I signed a contract with Saburov. The Director was then in very friendly relations with Mlle Rosati, and, according to agreement, had granted her a benefit performance, and obligated himself to reserve for this day the first performance of a new grand ballet, the composition of which was entrusted to me.

Having sketched out a plan for the ballet, I left for Paris, to discuss the details with M. Saint-Georges.[2] I spent three weeks there, working every day with the composer, and when we had finished working out the whole programme of my ballet, *The Daughter of Pharaoh*, I returned to St Petersburg. On the way back I visited the Egyptian Museum in Berlin, with the tombs of the Pharaohs, which had Egyptian paintings on them. All these Egyptian paintings depicted the figure in profile, because at that period artists did not know how to draw it in any other way.

I studied all these pictures attentively, but naturally I surmised that the profile positions were the result of the insufficiently developed craftsmanship of the painters, and did not compel the artists in *The Daughter of Pharaoh* to dance only in profile. Although their painters drew people in a certain way, the Egyptians certainly walked as we do, that is, in a straight direction. Conceited ignoramuses must have their brains twisted, to force people to walk and dance always in profile, as has been done by Teliakovsky's[3] creatures. Striving for new effects, they ignore the requirements of good taste.

During my absence, the Director had a disagreement with Mlle Rosati, and for several months I waited in vain for the order to proceed with rehearsals for the new ballet. Two months before the close of the season Mlle Rosati, convinced that the Director was intentionally forgetting about the approach of her benefit, and the new ballet, spoke to me.

"You will not have time enough to stage a new ballet. It is only two months until Lent. Will you be so kind as to come with me to see the Director, and explain this?"

I went with her to see M. Saburov, and we sent in our cards. The servant returned and said that His Excellency requested me to come into his office alone.

I entered and found the Director in his dressing gown, as

usual. From the day he began his duties, he received all the artists, men and women, in this costume. He had even had a "little" unpleasantness with one of the lady artists, about this. His Excellency was carried away and did not notice that the skirt of his dressing gown had fallen open, but the artist noticed. She also observed that the Director had nothing on under the dressing gown, and gave him a resounding slap in the face. As you see, in those days also, as in our time, there were directors who were willing to swallow physical punishment. This did not stop Saburov from continuing his directorial functions. In our day, this has aided advancement, and probably in remembrance of the saying "One beaten person is worth two unbeaten", the manager of the Moscow office has been made Director of the Imperial Theatres.

Of course, the Director's dressing gown did not shock me.

"M. Petipa! Why have you and Mlle Rosati come to see me?"

"To remind Your Excellency about the production of the ballet which must be given at her benefit."

"We cannot even consider a new ballet. We have neither the time nor the money for it."

"Will you be so kind, Your Excellency, as to give her this unpleasant news yourself? She is waiting in the salon."

"I can't receive her in my dressing gown, can I?"

"If you grant her request, she will not mind."

I went into the salon, and saying nothing to the ballerina about the Director's decision, I waited with her for his appearance. He came out almost immediately after me, in his elegant green dressing gown, and hardly greeting her, asked to what he owed the pleasure of seeing her.

"I have come, Your Excellency, to discuss the ballet which M. Petipa is to stage for my benefit."

"Unfortunately I am forced to inform you, Madame, that at the moment we do not have the money to stage such a big ballet."

"But indeed, Your Excellency, this was stipulated in my contract," fumed Rosati.

"I know, Madame! We will recompense you so liberally that you will have nothing to regret."

"Permit me to point out to you, *M. le Directeur*, that artists who enjoy a certain renown appreciate honours more than money."

"Perhaps, Madame; but unpleasant as it is for me, I can only repeat to you that because of unforseen circumstances *The Daughter of Pharaoh* cannot be staged this season."

"Then it seems to me that you do not attach any value to your signature."

"Madame!" The Director became very agitated. Trembling, in a fit of irritation he flung one leg over a chair; the dressing gown, of course, fell open. My pen refuses to describe what we saw.

"Do not forget, Madame, that you are speaking to a high official!"

Afraid to look up, Mlle Rosati cast her eyes down, and had to turn aside to keep from laughing.

The visibility of His Excellency's person did not help to increase his prestige, and I considered it my duty to hurry to his assistance and screen him from view, because it was plainly to be seen that his whole body was literally shaking with rage.

Then Saburov, too, noticed what his treacherous dressing-gown had done, and quickly took his foot off the chair, and began to mutter:

"Excuse me, Madame, excuse me!"

This critical incident quickly cooled their tempers, and the Director turned to ask me:

"M. Petipa, can you stage this ballet in six weeks?"

To produce such a big and difficult ballet in six weeks was not an easy task. Fearing to assume such a heavy responsibility, and yet not wishing to injure the interests of the ballerina, I did not know what to reply. Observing my

THE DAUGHTER OF PHARAOH 53

hesitation, Mlle Rosati quickly stepped to my side and began to nudge me with her elbow. Saburov, also, noticed her behaviour.

"Why have you moved so close to M. Petipa, Madame?"

"Both of us together are not enough to stand up to Your Excellency!" I said, coming to the assistance of the ballerina.

"I see that you are a diplomat, M. Petipa. But answer my question. Will you be ready?"

"I will."

"Then be careful! Remember that you have promised."

"In any case, Your Excellency, I hope that this cannot furnish a motive for banishing me from Russia!" I jokingly replied.

Right there before us, the Director called his secretary and ordered him to notify the regisseur, Marcel.

"Write to him, and have him inform everyone that to-morrow M. Petipa will start the rehearsals of his ballet *The Daughter of Pharaoh*. Let him immediately order everything necessary from the machinists, set designers, and costumers."

And what else? Sufficient money was found, of course, and work progressed rapidly. In six weeks the posters announced the first performance of *The Daughter of Pharaoh*. This ballet had an enormous success, and we gave it the entire Easter week, matinees and evenings.

The Director's excuse of "no money" had been a hollow pretext – this none of us had doubted. Everyone knew that the question of the government money bothered the theatrical officials very little, from the lowest to the very highest. It was no secret from anybody, for example, where and how material for costumes was purchased.

In St Petersburg, at that time, there was a very fashionable English store, where everything sold for three times as much, and where they depended entirely on customers who did not know the value of money. And this was where the office of the Imperial Theatres bought costume materials, paying a rouble or more per yard for materials which could easily be obtained for 20 kopecks in any other store. But the officials used to go to the English store and get expensive bracelets, earrings and other things for their favourites, without paying a penny for them. Those somewhat lower in rank had no aversion to accepting money in cash, also, at Easter time and on New Year's Day.

With the conclusion of the winter season, Mlle Rosati's contract also terminated. This season was her swan song; she left for Paris, and never appeared on the stage again.

The role of Aspicia in *The Daughter of Pharaoh* was given to my wife, and it became one of her finest roles; the public always gave her a magnificent reception in it.

NOTES TO CHAPTER IX

(1) Carolina Rosati (née Galletti, 1826-1905) made her début in St Petersburg on September 13, 1859, in *Jovita*. Perrot did, as Petipa recalled, retire at just about this time, but *Jovita* was staged not by him, but by Arthur Saint-Léon, after Joseph Mazilier. Rosati danced in Russia for three seasons, and Aspicia in *The Daughter of Pharaoh*, presented January 18, 1862, was the last role she created.

(2) Jules Henri Vernoy de Saint-Georges (1799-1875) was one of the most prolific dramatists of his century, providing libretti for innumerable operas, operettas, and ballets. He collaborated with Théophile Gautier and Jean Coralli (and, unofficially, with Jules Perrot) on *Giselle*, and with Marie Taglioni on *Le Papillon*. With Marius Petipa, he devised the plots for *The Daughter of Pharaoh*, *Camargo*, and *Le Roi Candaule*. For two letters from Saint-Georges to Petipa, see Chapter XIII.

(3) V. A. Teliakovsky, Petipa's bitterest enemy, was the Director of the Imperial Theatres at the time these memoirs were written. A former colonel of the Imperial Guard, and later head of the Moscow office of the Imperial Theatres, he was appointed Director in 1901, to replace Prince Sergei Volkonsky (see Chapter XI). The "conceited ignoramus" who had people "walk and

dance always in profile" was undoubtedly Alexander Gorsky, a protégé of Teliakovsky's, who had hurt Petipa deeply by re-choreographing his beloved *Daughter of Pharaoh* when he produced it in Moscow.

CHAPTER X

FRUITFUL YEARS

FOLLOWING M. Saburov, Count Borch was appointed Director, but death removed him after his very first year in this post. His successor was Gedeonov, the son of the former Director. He understood theatrical affairs very well, and was familiar with every detail, but his already unsteady nerves could not bear the strain of activity demanded by conscientious attention to the duties which he took upon himself. During this period I staged two new ballets: *Le Roi Candaule* and *Mlada*.

At the death of Gedeonov, Baron Kister was appointed as Director of the Imperial Theatres. With this appointment there began an era of economy in production. Baron Kister did not like to spend money for this purpose, and insisted that old materials be used. "To renovate, to repair, to touch up" became the only occupation of all the ateliers, during the staging of new works.

Occasionally this stinginess had sad consequences. I staged a ballet called *The Daughter of the Snows*, in which the well-known and wonderful dancer, Mlle Vazem,[1] appeared. In this ballet we had to change the scenery very rapidly, when the winter landscape changed to summer and back again.

At the second performance of *The Daughter of the Snows*, this change turned into a complete fiasco. The wings, as well as the set at the back, cracked, toppled over, and broke in pieces. The machinist at that time was Legat, a relative of the Legat family of ballet dancers. The disastrous incident of the scenery so affected him, that he lost his reason right there on the stage.

Apparently this illness was hereditary in the Legat family,

and I sorrowfully recalled this case when, not long ago, we went to bury the talented dancer Sergei Legat.[2]

The Emperor Alexander II, with several members of his family, deigned to attend one of the ballet performances at the theatre. During the intermission, over a cup of tea, speaking of different ballets, he recalled with pleasure having seen in his childhood the charming ballet *La Fille du Danube*, with Mlle Taglioni in the title role. His Majesty said that he would very much like to see it again, in order to reawaken his childhood impressions.

The Director of the Theatre, Baron Kister, who was sitting in the adjacent box, overheard His Majesty's words. He hurried to the stage and summoned me, to tell me what His Majesty had said.

"I would like to give His Majesty a pleasant surprise, by staging *La Fille du Danube*."

"A splendid idea, Your Excellency."

"Do you know this ballet, Petipa?"

"I have heard a lot about it, but have never seen it."

"Then come to see me tomorrow morning, and we will discuss it."

On the following day, of course, I was in the Director's office, and expressed my opinion on the difficulties of staging a ballet so long forgotten. I thought that it would be absolutely necessary to have new costumes and scenery.

"It is not necessary," he replied, "We will do without. We can stage it very well, by freshening up the old scenery and using it again."

"I beg your pardon, Your Excellency, but you are forgetting that in childhood, everything seems beautiful. Now, it is a different matter. To please His Majesty, this ballet will have to be superbly staged."

"No, no!" insisted the Baron, thinking of economy before everything else.

"Be careful, Your Excellency, that such a production does not anger His Majesty, instead of pleasing him!"

"Never mind, Petipa, just send me tomorrow a list of the settings and everything you will have to use in this ballet."

Attending the first performance, His Majesty came back stage during the intermission, and honoured me by speaking to me personally, in the following words:

"M. Petipa, the dances you have staged are charming, but in the most miserable country theatre, did you ever see such rags instead of costumes and scenery?"

I bowed in silent agreement, and His Majesty returned to his box.

Very shortly after this, Baron Kister was replaced by M. Vsevolojsky,[3] who occupied the post of Director of the Imperial Theatres for seventeen years.

Not long before this, there also occurred a great change in my personal life. I had aided greatly in the success of my first wife. I had done everything I could to help her attain the highest position on the ballet stage, but in our domestic life we were unable to live long in peace and harmony. Our differences in character, and perhaps the false self-esteem of both of us, soon made a compatible life impossible. My first wife died in Pyatigorsk in 1875, and in the following year I first learned what is meant by domestic happiness, and a pleasant family hearth. Having married Lubov Leonidova, the daughter of the artist Leonidov, I learned the value of a kind and loving wife, and if I am lively and healthy today, in spite of my advanced age, I dare say that I owe it entirely to the love and care of my wife, who to this day gives me affection and attention and complete happiness.

During the long years of Vsevolojsky's management, all the artists, without exception, adored their noble, kind, cultured director. This kindest of men was a real courtier, in the best sense of the word. I had the honour to work with him frequently, and in addition to everything else he possessed great talent for making sketches that were full of taste and intelligence, for operas and ballets. With what regret, with what pangs of the heart do I recall those happy days before the production of the unfortunate and, for me, fatal ballet, *The Magic Mirror*, the designs for which were hideously created by some woman,[4] who even now is connected with the Imperial Theatres, to their misfortune. For some reason, she also imagines herself a painter, and sticks her nose into everything, arranging and commanding. The costumes for the dancers in this particular ballet were made in such a way that the hats fell to their noses, and costumes more monstrous and ludicrous it is difficult to imagine.

During those never-to-be-forgotten seventeen years of Vsevolojsky's management, every one of my ballets was successful, and I staged many:

The Sleeping Beauty	*The Four Seasons*
Cinderella	*Ruses d'Amour*
Swan Lake	*Harlequinade*
Bluebeard	*Les Elèves de Dupré*
Raymonda	*Don Quixote*
The Halt of the Cavalry	*Camargo*
The Awakening of Flora	*Nénuphar*

Day and Night
(staged on the occasion of the coronation of the Emperor
Alexander III)

The Pearl
(for the coronation of the Emperor Nicholas II)

La Bayadère
The Caprices of the Butterfly
The Magic Pills
The Talisman
The Vestal
The King's Command
The Grasshopper Musician
A Midsummer Night's Dream
Les Caprices de l'Amour
The Tulip of Haarlem
The Nutcracker, etc., etc.

That was a wonderful time, when art flourished on the Imperial stages of St Petersburg, and all the artists said good-bye to M. Vsevolojsky with real tears in their eyes, when he gave up the post of Director.

But I suffered the most of all from this separation, feeling an irreparable loss in the departure of this never-to-be-forgotten Director. The creation and staging of a big ballet presents enormous difficulties; in outlining the scenario or programme, one must think of all the individual roles; having completed the story and pantomimic part of the ballet, one must invent and create the appropriate dances, *pas*, and variations, and make them conform to the music. This work becomes pleasant when one finds in the director such a well-informed and gifted adviser as was M. Vsevolojsky, or when one works with a composer of genius, such as Tschaikovsky.

All the decors, costumes, and accessories, which conformed to the style, period, and character of the subject, were devised by M. Vsevolojsky. He himself made the sketches, which naturally lightened the problems of everyone connected with the production. The Director knew how to use for the ballet the power and genius of the great Russian composer Tschaikovsky, who wrote three such works as *The Sleeping Beauty*, *Swan Lake*, and *The Nutcracker*. Under the same Director, the talented composer Glazounov also wrote for the ballet. He gave us *Raymonda*, *Ruses d'Amour*, and *The Four Seasons*. This was a comparatively short time ago, and these gifted composers found in me a worthy colleague, a person far removed from envy, and full of sincere respect.

One is able to judge what our relations were, by the following letter from the genius, Tschaikovsky. Here is what he wrote me before the production of our ballet *The Sleeping Beauty*:

"Tiflis, 26 April, 1889.

"Dear and highly esteemed colleague!

I have almost completed the sketches for the fifth scene of the ballet *The Sleeping Beauty*. Everything will be finished not later than June first. But it would be interesting to know if what I read in one Russian newspaper is true. It announced that the production of our ballet has been postponed until the season of 1890-91, and that in this coming season they intend to revive the ballet *The Little Hunchbacked Horse*. The thing is, that if this news is correct, then I would not have to hurry so much with the orchestration of the ballet, having a whole year, or even more, for its arrangement; if this is only a false alarm, I must get to work immediately, in order to have the score of the entire ballet ready by September. Be so kind, dear M. Petipa, as to notify me if the management has really decided to postpone our ballet until the season of 1890-91. I am leaving here in a few days, and around May 10th expect to be already settled in my country place. About May 25th, I expect to come to St Petersburg for two days, and if I find you still there, I will have the pleasure of seeing you.

Your truly devoted,

P. Tschaikovsky"[5]

On December 6, 1900, another well-known composer, Glazounov, wrote to me:

"Dear M. Petipa,

I deeply regret that I have to write instead of seeing you, because I have been ill for several days. I have just received from Moscow a letter from N. Koreschenko,[6] whom I have already introduced to you. He asks me to inquire whether you will give him two hours on Sunday, December 10, in order to discuss the ballet which has been commissioned from him by the management of the Maryinsky Theatre. In expectation of your kind reply, which I will communicate to M. Koreschenko by telegraph, I take the opportunity to express once more my most sincere feeling of devotion.

A. Glazounov"

It is understandable that with such composers, and such a Director as M. Vsevolojsky, the majority of my ballet productions had an enormous success, and ballet flourished in St Petersburg. The ballet *Swan Lake* had been performed first in Moscow, and there it had no success at all. Knowing of this, I went to the Director and told him that I could not admit that Tschaikovsky's music was the cause of the failure; the fault lay not in the music, but in the staging of the ballet, in the dances. I asked the Director to permit me to make use of Tschaikovsky's score, and to produce the ballet in St Petersburg, utilizing the subject in my own way. M. Vsevolojsky agreed with me immediately, we got in touch with Tschaikovsky, and we produced *Swan Lake* with enormous success.[7]

Tschaikovsky was absolutely delighted, and said that he would never compose ballets for anyone except Petipa. But to whom were we indebted for this opportunity, if not to M. Vsevolojsky?

NOTES TO CHAPTER X

(1) Ekaterina Vazem (1848-1937), a cold and brilliant technician, noted for her impeccable pirouettes and steel-like *pointes*, was one of Petipa's favourite ballerinas. Between 1864 and 1884 she danced leading roles in many of his ballets, including *Camargo*, *The Bandits*, *Roxana*, *La Bayadère*, and his revival of Philippe Taglioni's *La Fille du Danube*.

(2) Sergei Legat, brother of the noted dancer and teacher Nicholas Legat, committed suicide during the revolution of 1905, at the height of his career. A number of dancers, including Michel Fokine, Tamara Karsavina and Anna Pavlova, had declared a strike, demanding higher salaries and a voice in the artistic management of the Imperial Ballet. Torn between loyalty to the theatre and loyalty to his comrades, Sergei Legat cut his throat. The tragic story is told in Tamara Karsavina's *Theatre Street*, Chapter XVI.

(3) Ivan Alexandrovich Vsevolojsky (1835-1909), under whom Petipa enjoyed his most fruitful creative period, was Director of the Imperial Theatres from 1881 to 1899.

(4) The costumes for *The Magic Mirror* were designed by Mme Guria Longuinovna Teliakovskaya, wife of the Director. A close friend of the painters Golovine and Korovine, she considered herself an authority on modern art, and enjoyed collaborating on her husband's productions.

(5) *The Sleeping Beauty* was not postponed, but received its first performance in January, 1890. The letter reproduced here gives little idea of the very close collaboration between Petipa and the great composer. Before Tschaikovsky composed a note of music, Petipa had planned the ballet in the most minute detail, suggesting not only the rhythm, orchestration, dramatic character and exact length of each number, but even breaking them up into measures. For example, Petipa's notes on the conversation between the King and the Master of Ceremonies, in Act I, gave strict instructions for the pattern of the music:

"No. 4, the King asks: 'What happened?' Give 4 measures for the question and 4 for the answer . . .

'Where are you taking them?' – 4 measures.

Answer – 'To prison' – 4 measures.

Question – 'What have they done?' – 4 measures.

Answer – points to knitting needles – 4 measures."

Later, during rehearsals, it was found that Tschaikovsky had not written enough music for the unfolding of the cyclorama, when the Lilac Fairy leads the Prince to the enchanted castle. At the choreographer's request, Tschaikovsky inserted a number of bars, which are still known as the "yard music".

The magnificent score and an excellent cast of dancers, including Carlotta Brianza, Paul Gerdt, Enrico Cecchetti, Varvara Nikitina and Marie Mariusovna Petipa (his daughter), inspired Petipa to create for *The Sleeping Beauty* choreographic designs of such masterful simplicity and beauty that they have survived for more than half a century. It would be difficult to name any dance more completely expressive of its theme and its music than the great Rose Adagio, nor any Pas de Deux of more elegance and grandeur than that of Aurora and Prince Desire in the last act. Each of the variations for the fairies, in the Prologue, is a miniature masterpiece.

Even the comic interlude, Puss in Boots and the White Cat,

owes much of its distinctive musical quality to Petipa's imagination, for he suggested to Tschaikovsky: "Repeated mewing, denoting caressing and clawing. For the end – clawing and screaming of the male cat. It should begin 3/4 amoroso, and end in 3/4 with accelerated mewing." (These excerpts from Petipa's notes are from Yuri Slonimsky's essay on Marius Petipa, translated by Anatole Chujoy and published in *Dance Index*, Vol. VI, Nos. 5 and 6. This study contains further interesting information about Petipa's collaboration with Tschaikovsky and Alexander Glazounov, as well as with the lesser composers who wrote ballets for him.)

(6) Arseny Nikolaevich Koreschenko (1870-1921), a pianist and composer, had been commissioned to provide the score for Petipa's ballet *The Magic Mirror*, which was to prove a disastrous failure, and the last full-scale production of the veteran choreographer.

(7) It was in 1877 that *Swan Lake* was first produced in Moscow, with choreography by one Julius Reisinger, later revised by J. Hansen. In 1888 the Prague Opera presented the second act alone, with Giulietta Paltrinieri-Bergrovà as Odette and August Berger, who did the choreography, as Prince Siegfried.

Several more years passed before Petipa conceived the plan of staging *Swan Lake*. While he may have consulted with the great composer about the new use of his score, it must have been his plans, and not the finished ballet, which delighted Tschaikovsky, for he died in the autumn of 1893, before the new version had been produced.

Although Petipa planned the choreography of the entire ballet, he left the construction of the dances in the second and fourth acts, the famous scenes of the swans by the lake, to his assistant, Lev Ivanov, while he himself staged the first and third acts, including the Peasant Pas de Trois and the brilliant divertissements in the ballroom.

The second act only, with Pierina Legnani as Odette, was presented at a concert in memory of the composer, on February 17, 1894. The premiere of the complete ballet, in the version still familiar to us in the Royal Ballet production, took place at the

THE SLEEPING BEAUTY, THE PROLOGUE
A Scene from The Royal Ballet's Production

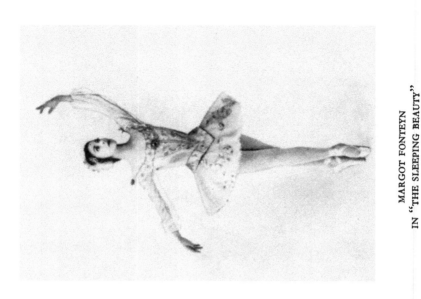

MARGOT FONTEYN
IN "THE SLEEPING BEAUTY"

CARLOTTA BRIANZA
WHO CREATED "THE SLEEPING BEAUTY"

Maryinsky Theatre on January 15, 1895. Legnani danced the dual role of Odette-Odile, and it was to display her prodigious virtuosity that the famous 32 fouettés were included in the coda of the Grand Pas de Deux in Act III.

CHAPTER XI

THE COLONEL-OF-THE-ARTS

As it turned out, Vsevolojsky had a worthy successor in Prince Volkonsky.[1] Having been a performing artist himself (the Prince had often taken part in court spectacles at the Hermitage), loving art in general, and the theatre in particular, the new Director devoted himself enthusiastically to his new duties. But this very enthusiasm was dangerous: planning many reforms, he wanted to execute them at once, and to bring about a new order immediately, instead of by degrees. He gave neither himself nor others sufficient time to weigh and consider matters; thanks to this haste, there were of course many mistakes. But the Prince himself realized this after a few weeks; he came to the conclusion that in order to reach the goal it would be necessary to go forward gradually, *pianissimo*.

Prince Volkonsky commissioned me to do a new ballet, advising me to take the theme from Pushkin's *The Magic Mirror*. The score for this ballet was commissioned from the composer Koreschenko. The latter had been introduced to me by the gifted maestro Glazounov, whose recommendation was an absolute guarantee of the talent and craftsmanship of the man with whom I was to work.

We had hardly started the first rehearsals of the new ballet when we were thunder-struck by the announcement of the retirement of Prince Volkonsky, who relinquished his post because of a trifling incident, which hurt him cruelly.[2]

In causing the retirement of Prince Volkonsky, the originator of this affair unfortunately did much harm to the St Petersburg ballet, and dealt a severe blow to all the Imperial Theatres, because unfortunately his place fell to a certain

Colonel Teliakovsky, who had previously managed the Moscow office. I will not stop to explain how and why this officer became "manager" of the theatres, supervising art after running the household of a regiment. At the time, this appointment called forth unanimously adverse criticism in all the papers.[3]

The retirement of Prince Volkonsky was a fatal blow for the Imperial Theatres, because this skilled, cultivated, kind person, honest in all his dealings, was replaced by an individual by no means able to promote the flowering of art on the Imperial stages.

Almost at once, I personally found M. Teliakovsky to be my bitterest enemy. He stopped at nothing. I was very soon to learn the direct strategy of this Colonel-of-the-Arts, for in fighting against people who did not please him, and whom, for some reason, he wished to discard, he was by no means scrupulous in his choice of weapons. He is a follower of the "new" school. Unfortunately, under his régime, works in which virtue triumphs, and evil is chastised, are completely forgotten. Now, on the contrary, evil triumphs viciously.

The first attack. On the occasion of the visit of the President of the French Republic, Émile Loubet, a gala performance was given at Peterhof. Everything went perfectly. The august personages and the distinguished guest expressed their fullest pleasure. Three days later, I was summoned to see M. Lappa, the head of the theatre office, who gave me some more than distressing news. He had a list of all the artists who had participated in the gala performance for President Loubet, who wished, as is customary, to honour them with gifts. As the oldest representative of the St Petersburg stage, who had earned distinction by serving for fifty-five years, and was, besides, a Frenchman by origin, my name had been placed at the head of the list. But the new Director had unceremoniously crossed it out.

It is not difficult to imagine how such an affront, delivered before the entire company, affected me. During fifty-five years of service I had been accustomed only to praise and acclamation from the Czars, the Ministers, the Directors, the press and the public. I could not stand it, and for the first time I permitted myself to complain to the Minister of the Court, Baron Fredericks.

I found a more than kind reception. When I had explained to the Minister the distressing occurrence which had brought me to see him, he replied: "I will investigate this matter, M. Petipa!"

The affair, however, was permitted to die down. Nevertheless Baron Fredericks was able to compensate for it by another means: shortly after my benefit, the office of the Imperial Theatres informed me, through an official document, that His Majesty had expressed the desire that I should remain as Ballet Master until the end of my days, with a salary of 9,000 roubles. This decree of His Majesty the Emperor I owe entirely to the efforts of the Minister, Baron Fredericks.

The second attack. On the day of my jubilee benefit, the corps de ballet presented me with a wreath, and naturally wished to give it to me with the curtain open, in view of the public. Mr Director Teliakovsky gave orders to his appointee, Krupensky, who in turn ordered the assistant regisseur, Usachev, not to permit the curtain to be raised, or the wreath to be presented to me before the audience.

Never before on our stage has there been such behaviour on the part of the management towards a person celebrating his jubilee. In spite of the efforts of Usachev, who barred our way to the stage, Mlle Trefilova[4] and the other dancers revolted against such harsh orders, pushed aside the obedient functionary of the Director, and literally dragged me by the arms out onto the stage, where the wreath was presented to the accompaniment of loud and prolonged applause, and shouts of "Bravo, Petipa! Bravo!"

A few days later I met M. Teliakovsky, and he asked me, with hypocritical sympathy:

"Is it possible, M. Petipa, that someone tried to prevent the presentation of your wreath, with the curtain open?"

"You should know best, Your Excellency, because the orders came from you!" I could not hold back.

After so many years of service it is not easy, you will agree, to be the victim of such baseness, and to find oneself obliged to fight against such low, contemptible tricks.

At one of the rehearsals in the theatre school, a certain youth suddenly appeared, and you can picture my astonishment when he was introduced to me as M. Krupensky, especially engaged to establish order in the ballet troupe, and to assign roles. I could not reconcile myself to the idea that a young man without the slightest comprehension of the art of choreography should be assigned to give orders and advice to a man who has devoted sixty years of his life to this business.

A few more days passed, and I learned that according to instructions from our military Director, this layman had formed a special committee, in which Mlle Preobrajenska,[5] my daughter Marie, the Legat brothers and a few other artists were to participate, under his chairmanship.

It was suggested to me that I join the staff of this committee, but I refused point-blank, finding it impossible that the artists themselves should form a committee for the assignment of roles. There is no doubt, as long experience has proved, that they will always divide the pie between themselves, occasionally leaving some crumbs for the students and younger artists. Under such a committee, it would be difficult for any dancers to make places for themselves in ballet, without special patronage.

The incompetence of Krupensky was aggravated by his rudeness: appearing at a rehearsal, where he understood about as much as a certain animal about oranges,[6] he would sit down at a table, cross his legs, and acknowledge the greetings of the dancers with a slight nod of the head. I do not know where he was brought up, but in my old age it is hard to reconcile myself with such decadent manners, which, from childhood, I had believed were found only in taverns or in amusement establishments of the lowest order. So began the "innovations" of M. Teliakovsky.

I was obliged to become familiar with another feature of this newest youthful school. When it was time to rehearse *The Daughter of Pharaoh*, I was "asked", according to the orders of the Director, to throw out of the corps de ballet all the dancers who were old and ugly. In order to avoid taking any responsibility for such a step, I sent the Director a list of the dancers previously used in *The Daughter of Pharaoh*, placing in another row the names of young dancers with whom the Director could, at his own discretion, replace those no longer in their first youth. For some reason he gave up the idea, and sent orders that I was to leave everything as it had been before. This, of course, I did with pleasure.

A few weeks later, M. Krupensky slipped into the Director's office, searched for my list, unceremoniously pocketed it, and began showing it to the elderly dancers.

"See how M. Petipa refers to you. He can't tolerate you, and wants to have you thrown out."

It is not necessary to explain that according to the rules of the theatre, no one ever tells the employees what is discussed by the people who are in charge of any part of the administration. This incident alone reveals the moral fibre of the Director's young favourite.

The following incident will demonstrate how far the present Director has gone in his strivings for "innovations" on the stage, even when they have been contrary to common sense and the first requirements of art.

Many years ago, I was commissioned to stage a Caucasian dance, the lezghinka, for Glinka's opera *Russlan and Ludmilla*. Not knowing the Caucasus, and not having the proper understanding of the characteristic peculiarities of the dances of that region, I did not consider myself qualified to create the national dance according to my own fantasy. I asked an officer acquaintance to bring me four Caucasian dancers from his regiment. He fulfilled my request; the dashing Circassians performed the lezghinka for me several times. I watched attentively and studied all their steps, their style of dancing, and only after completely mastering all this, staged the lezghinka in *Russlan and Ludmilla*. M. Bekefi and my daughter Marie had a colossal success in it, repeating it several times at the unanimous insistence of the audience.

Not long ago, on the occasion of the celebration of its two-hundredth performance, Teliakovsky decided to renovate this opera, in spite of the fact that it pained him "to lose time" in staging the work of the great Russian composer, to the detriment of Wagner. The Director discovered that the national character dance was "antiquated", and ordered Shiraev,[7] the ballet master, to create some "new" lezghinka. Shiraev quite reasonably observed to Teliakovsky that in his time M. Petipa had staged this dance, not according to his own imagination, but as the Circassions danced it.

"Never mind," replied the Director (?) of the Imperial Theatres, "that is not important. Create something else. Even if it is worse, at least it will be new."

At the general rehearsal of *Russlan* I was in one of the boxes, in the capacity of a simple spectator, to enjoy once more Glinka's wonderful music. On seeing the "lezghinka" which Shiraev had created, I could only throw up my hands in despair. What was danced on the stage had nothing in common with the Circassians or the Caucasus. I had hardly finished expressing my opinion to those seated in the box with me, when M. Krupensky appeared with an invitation to visit the box of the Director, who wished to speak to me.

I went. M. Teliakovsky addressed me with the request that I change the dance Shiraev had created, a little, to correct it.

"But why did you throw out the lezghinka that I arranged? Indeed, M. Shiraev told you that the lezghinka which I staged for *Russlan* was authentic, and drew tremendous applause, almost an ovation, from the audience."

"I thought that he would create something a little more novel."

"Then order my lezghinka danced. I cannot invent anything better, because the lezghinka I staged was created by the Lezghins."

Then the Director decided to keep the lezghinka created by Shiraev, which had nothing to do with the Caucasian national dance. Of course, it failed gloriously. When I returned to my box, I could only say:

"It is a misfortune to have anything to do with such directors!"

NOTES TO CHAPTER XI

(1) Prince Serge Volkonsky (1860-1937), Director of the Imperial Theatres from 1899 to 1902, chose Sergei Diaghilev as his assistant, and thus influenced the whole future course of Diaghilev's career. The two had an unfortunate disagreement when Diaghilev wished to be given absolute authority over a production of the ballet *Sylvia*, and Diaghilev resigned. The two were reconciled many years later. During the revolution, in 1917, Prince Volkonsky fled to the United States, where he died twenty years later.

(2) The ballerina Mathilda Kschessinska had great influence at court, and it was one of her whims which indirectly brought about Volkonsky's resignation. In a revival of the ballet *Camargo* she had been told to wear an authentic eighteenth-century costume, with bulky paniers. She refused to dance in the paniers, and appeared at the first performance without them. The next day a notice was posted on the theatre bulletin board, stating that Mlle Kschessinska had been fined for modifying her costume, against the express orders of the Director.

Two days later Volkonsky was summoned to appear before

the Czar and explain what had happened. When Volkonsky had finished his account of the affair, the Czar commanded that Mlle Kschessinska's fine be remanded, and that the announcement of its cancellation be posted publicly. Volkonsky submitted to the wishes of the Czar, but said that under the circumstances he would be forced to hand in his resignation. The Czar asked him to think it over. However, when Volkonsky reached his home, after this same audience with the Czar, he found already waiting for him a message stating that his resignation had been regretfully accepted.

(3) *Mir Isskustva* (*The World of Art*), the famous magazine edited by Diaghilev, Leon Bakst, Alexander Benois and other members of Diaghilev's circle, was particularly violent in its attacks on Teliakovsky's early experiments, although several of these artists later became his collaborators.

(4) Vera Trefilova (1875-1943) had graduated from the Imperial School in 1894, and was already a prominent soloist. Years later she was to dance Aurora in Diaghilev's production of *The Sleeping Princess*, in London.

(5) Olga Preobrajenska had graduated as a member of the corps de ballet in 1889, and had gradually risen through the ranks until, by 1898, she was dancing ballerina roles. In more recent years her Paris studio produced such excellent dancers as Irina Baronova, Tamara Toumanova, and Tatiana Riabouchinska. At the age of eighty-seven, she was still actively teaching.

(6) "He knows as much as a pig understands about oranges" is an old Russian saying.

Petipa was not the only person to suffer from the ruthless machinations of the unscrupulous Alexander Dimitrievich Krupensky. Alexander Benois, in his *Reminiscences of the Russian Ballet*, describes his difficulties with Krupensky, then head of the production department of the Maryinsky Theatre. Although Krupensky, to further his own ambitions, had been instrumental in arranging for the production of the ballet *Le Pavillon d'Armide*, on which Benois was collaborating with Michel Fokine, he later proved treacherous and tried to sabotage all their plans.

It was Krupensky, too, who called attention to the brevity of

Nijinsky's tunic in *Giselle*, in 1911, on the famous occasion which resulted in Nijinsky's resignation from the Imperial Theatre. (Benois, *op. cit.*, pp. 317-18).

(7) Alexander Victorovich Shiraev, who had graduated from the Imperial School in 1885, was an assistant ballet master.

CHAPTER XII

REFORMS AND INTRIGUES

I HAVE never opposed reforms, but reasonable reforms. All my life I have believed that the young element must be given a chance, but they must be talented and capable people, and incompetents should not be pushed ahead just because they have influential friends.

I have always believed that before appearing in public, an artist should pass an examination before a committee of specialists, capable of judging whether he is ready to appear on the stage. It is not right to force the public, who pay quite enough for their seats, to suffer the performances of incompetent or inexperienced students.

Not so thinks M. Krupensky, who himself came straight from school to guide the affairs of the St Petersburg ballet, which until then had been considered the criterion, in this field, in all of Europe.

M. Andreyanov,[1] who just graduated from the theatre school last year, and still has much to learn, has been appointed teacher of the boys' classes. The fate of the students of this student is not to be envied. Such a graduating class is sure to be worthless anywhere, and M. Krupensky's arrangement can only lead to a complete absence of skilled artists, within ten years.

Two years ago Mlle Eugenia Sokolova,[2] who had earlier served as *première danseuse*, and had always distinguished herself by her special grace and talent, was appointed professor of the class of perfection. Pavlova II,[3] Sedova, and Trefilova studied with her and made enormous progress under her direction. The Director found this superfluous, discharged her, and appointed as professor, in her place, one of

75

his own creatures. Without touching on the knowledge and personality of this man, I can only say that he was completely unable to teach the dancers grace and charm, which can only be taught by a woman, and especially by someone like Mlle Sokolova, who was herself the personification of grace. Indeed, this method is accepted on all the outstanding ballet stages of Europe. In Paris this department is directed by Mlle Mauri,[3] who appeared for a long time on the stage of the Paris Opéra; in Milan, at La Scala, such classes were led by Mlle Beretta,[5] and in Berlin by the daughter of the late ballet master Taglioni.

From all these examples, it is not difficult to understand what Teliakovsky and Krupensky are looking for. They want only obedient servants, obliging creatures bowing before them, and occupying themselves with spying and denunciations. Capable and independent people, people with initiative and knowledge of their craft, cannot possibly work under such directors. Such people would not take the advice and kiss the hands of the unofficial queen of the Imperial Theatre [i.e., Mme Teliakovsky – L.M.], who considers herself an artist, and a big authority on theatrical matters. Under a cultured, intelligent and independent director one works better, and anyone who loves his work will think, labour, and try to study every angle during the production of a new work, worrying over the smallest detail.

I recall the production of the ballet *Don Quixote*. On the eve of the first performance of this big ballet of mine, I went to the cavalry grounds (on Semenovsky Place) and searched for a long time until I found a horse worthy of the role of Rosinante.

At the very first performance, the Grand Dukes came back stage to admire the horse with the drooping head, jutting ribs, and stiff back leg, answering exactly to Cervantes' description of him.

"Petipa!" the Grand Duke Constantine Nikolaievich

asked me, "Where did you get a horse which fills the role of Rosinante so perfectly?"

"I succeeded in finding him on the Semenovsky military grounds, Your Highness!"

"How much did you pay for him?"

"Nine roubles, Your Highness."

"A gift, Petipa! In him you have acquired a great actor to add to the personnel of your company."

My purchase of this horse really had an enormous success; on his appearance the entire audience broke into irrepressible laughter, and applauded a long time.

Later on, I will speak about what goes on during the production of ballets now. I still have several things to add concerning M. Teliakovsky's relations with me.

When rumours about the loathsome occurrences and intrigues against me finally reached the public, an interviewer called on the Director, pretending to seek the answers to several questions about me.

As soon as the conversation turned to M. Petipa, the reporter, in his newspaper, quoted M. Teliakovsky as saying:

"He is too old. He is over eighty, and his memory betrays him. Today he forgets what he said yesterday, and tomorrow he won't remember what was said today."

That I am old – that is true, but my memory, thank God, is still good. What better proof can I submit to the judgement of the public, than this book? It was after the amiable testimony by the youthful Colonel-Director, that I thought of writing my memoirs; and without any notes, without any diary, I have remembered and recalled all the outstanding events of my life, beginning with eight years of age. This, in parentheses; I return to the further conversation between the Director and the interviewer who arrived so opportunely.

"Why don't we have any more good choreographers?"

"The fault is M. Petipa's," replied M. Teliakovsky, untroubled by the monstrousness of such an intentionally deceitful statement, "as soon as we find a young and capable ballet master, he begins to persecute him."

All of my past activities, all my well-known relationships with my comrades and artists during many years of service, give me the full right to make an energetic protest, and to declare frankly that this is a lie, a lie, and a lie.

Formerly, every well-known ballet master began his career on second or even third-rate stages. But my pupil, Gorsky,[6] in spite of the fact that he had never, anywhere, staged a work of his own, was immediately honoured with an invitation to the Bolshoi Theatre of Moscow, in the capacity of ballet master. What else did M. Teliakovsky want? Plainly, what he wanted was for me to give up my place in Petersburg to this creature of his. He wanted M. Gorsky and his kind to stand at the head of the St Petersburg ballet. What arrogance! This is the only thing it is possible to say.

Along with me there served, as regisseur and second ballet master, M. Alexei Bogdanov, while the ballet masters were Lev Ivanov, Shiraev, Cecchetti, and the same M. Gorsky. I dare to state that in them I was preparing for myself successors who could replace me advantageously, at any time.

It is not my fault that M. Gorsky, to please his patron, followed another path, and in stealing my works began to put into them such "novelty" as can in no way serve to his advantage. In Moscow he staged my ballet *Don Quixote*, which had already had more than two hundred performances, and in order to present "something new" to please the new Director, he changed the names of the characters: the daughter of Pharaoh, Aspicia,[7] was changed to Binte-Tante, etc. Instead of one daughter of Pharaoh, there were three; why didn't he give him a round dozen, to please the young ballet public? How much talent do you suppose is necessary for such "innovations"? What a genius!

"What impertinence!" competent people can only say.

This same Gorsky, and other obliging followers of the

innovator-colonel, permitted themselves to cripple even the theme and subject of my ballet, just to give opportunities to the decadent painters who enjoyed the favour of the all-powerful lady who ruled the Imperial Theatre [Mme Telia-kovsky – L.M.]. In order to make a new decor for the bank of the Nile, they ruled out the fisherman's hut as superfluous. What was the result? In the scene where the Nubian King pursues and tries to capture Aspicia, she can run anywhere she wants, and there is no need for her to throw herself into the water. The effectiveness of the scene is lost, and the meaning of the story mutilated, but what does this matter to people who are trying to please only one self-confident, self-centred, obstinate person?

In 1903, although I was already very old, all the same I was able to create a one-act ballet for the Hermitage, *The Romance of the Rose and the Butterfly*, on the theme of M. V——, with music by Drigo. On seeing it all the artists, without exception, gave me an ovation, and I heard only: "M. Petipa, this is a little masterpiece!" Notwithstanding my advanced age, I am not absolutely dead, Mr Teliakovsky!

What didn't this Director do, to finish me? Since a clear example of it can further the purposes of my career, I must, for the protection of my reputation as a ballet-master, des-cribe in every detail the conditions under which I staged my last ballet, *The Magic Mirror*.

Already, during the rehearsals for this ballet, I was con-vinced that something was being plotted against me and my ballet, the commission for which had been given to M. Koreschenko and me by M. Volkonsky, and not by M. Teliakovsky. Mlle Kschessinska took an active part in this intrigue, revenging herself because at the benefit of her late father, I had not greeted him with a speech. I will not speak of that; it is not the business of the ballet master to shine with eloquence at every possible benefit. In this case, it was only because I had a sore throat and was unable to come forth with a public speech, that I did not do it. Mlle Kschessinska did not believe me, and in her resentment joined the camp of the colonel's followers, forgetting that I helped to create her artistic career, and that I was always ready to help her in everything which concerned her successes on the stage.

I will give one of her letters:

"Very dear and extremely kind M. Petipa,

You were so good as to answer my request with a promise to throw a friendly glance [in the original: *donner votre coup d'œil genial*] at my performance, when I rehearse my *pas* with Kyaksht.[8] On returning home, I realized that for Paris your inspiration is necessary, not just the fantasies of your obedient servant. Therefore, dear M. Petipa, I come to you with the request that you create for me a very, very pretty *pas de deux*, and I promise that you will not be ashamed of me. I have selected the music for this *pas* from the last act of *Coppélia*. I will still be here on Monday and Tuesday, and I hope that you will be kind enough to prepare the *pas* for me in these two days. Please accept in advance the gratitude or your devoted

Mathilda Kschessinska"

I learned the depth of this gratitude and devotion when the rehearsals of *The Magic Mirror* began.

To please the Director, the painter Golovine[9] had also joined the conspiracy. When, at the rise of the curtain, the decor of gnomes painted by this artist of the school of the décadents was seen for the first time, there resounded a unanimous roar of laughter.

At the end of the general rehearsal, I went to see the Director to implore him to let me stage some sort of old ballet for my benefit, and not to show the new creation to the public in such a deformed state. Suddenly, someone sneaked up behind me, covered my eyes with his hands, and shouted:

"Bravo, bravo, Petipa! This is the peak of perfection! This ballet will have an enormous success!"

ALICIA ALONSO
AS ODETTE IN "SWAN LAKE"

PIERINA LEGNANI
AS ODETTE IN "SWAN LAKE"

MARIA TALLCHIEF, YVONNE MOUNSEY AND PATRICIA WILDE IN THE
NEW YORK CITY BALLET'S PRODUCTION OF "SWAN LAKE"

"THE NUTCRACKER"
A SCENE FROM GEORGE BALANCHINE'S PRODUCTION,
FOR THE NEW YORK CITY BALLET

"No, Your Excellency, this ballet will be a triumphant failure."

"What are you saying? What are you saying? You are wrong, M. Petipa."

On the day of the first performance and of my benefit, the theatre was crammed full, and His Majesty and all the Imperial family were present in their box.

Anyone who was present at this performance will of course remember how venomously the audience laughed at everything that was shown to them – and it was entirely understandable. As I said above, the costumes and accessories, which were made after the sketches of the Director's closest colleague, were simply caricatures. The dancers, who were portraying the immortals, were dressed as nymphs, and so forth.

In a word, everything was horrible, and the pitiful costumes and scenery were not even ready. On the eve of my benefit I was asked to postpone it. Unfortunately I did not agree, taking the view that all the tickets had been sold, and it was impossible to treat the public so unceremoniously. I can still thank God that the Court, the public, and the press found it possible to exclude me from blame for the disgraceful production of the ballet, and acknowledged that my dances were successful.[10] All the same, the blow which the Director had given me was truly cruel and Macchiavellian.

NOTES TO CHAPTER XII

(1) Samuel Konstantinovich Andreyanov graduated from the Imperial School on June 1, 1902, and was appointed Professor of Dancing there on September 1, 1904.

(2) Eugenia Sokolova (1855-1926) created principal roles in many of Petipa's ballets, including *Roxana*, *the Beauty of Montenegro*, *Mlada*, *A Midsummer Night's Dream*, and *Pygmalion*.

(3) "Pavlova II" was, of course, the incomparable Anna Pavlova, who had graduated in 1899, and had in 1905 attained

G

the rank of ballerina. Apparently Petipa recognized her exceptional gifts, since he listed her first among Sokolova's outstanding
pupils. Julia Sedova was also a ballerina at the Maryinsky Theatre,
as was Vera Trefilova.

(4) Rosita Mauri (1849-1923), born in Spain, made her début
in Barcelona in 1868. A decade later she appeared at the Paris
Opéra, where she was to reign as *première danseuse étoile* for a
quarter of a century. She continued to teach there until 1920,
three years before her death.

(5) Caterina Beretta (1840-1911) danced at the Paris Opéra in
1855 and was prima ballerina at La Scala, Milan, for several
seasons (intermittently) between 1859 and 1877. In St Petersburg
her strength and virtuosity made a deep impression on the
Russian dancers trained in the softer, more gracious French
school. Beretta firmly believed that dancing was purely a matter
of physical prowess, and that expressive gesture meant little or
nothing in comparison with brilliance and speed. Pavlova,
Tefilova and Karsavina all went to Milan, at various times, to
study with her, and Karsavina gives a vivid picture of her as an
old woman, in *Theatre Street*, p. 173-6.

(6) Alexander Gorsky (1871-1924) had graduated from the
Imperial Ballet School in St Petersburg in 1889, and was named
solo dancer six years later. He was sent to Moscow to stage *The
Sleeping Beauty*, in 1899. Using the Stepanoff method of dance
notation, he reproduced Petipa's original choreography.

Except for *Clorinde*, staged for pupils of the Imperial School,
Gorsky's first original work was a new version of *Don Quixote*,
quite different from Petipa's, produced in Moscow on December
6, 1900. It was sharply attacked by the critics, provoking considerable controversy. Alexander Benois, writing as late as 1939
(*Reminiscenses of the Russian Ballet*, p. 222), described it as " . . . viti-
ated by the abhorrent lack of organization that is typical of
amateur performances. His 'novelties' consisted of making the
crowds on the stage bustle and move about fitfully and aim-
lessly . . . The dramatic possibilities and the dancers themselves
were depressed to a uniformly commonplace level. . . ." The first
St Petersburg performance of the Gorsky version of *Don Quixote*

MARGOT FONTEYN AND MICHAEL SOMES
IN THE ROYAL BALLET'S PRODUCTION
OF "SWAN LAKE"

SOLIANIKOV AND ROSINANTE IN "DON QUIXOTE"
AND ALEXANDER GORSKY

Two caricatures by S. and N. Legat

took place on January 20, 1902, and met with a decidedly unfavourable reception. In Moscow, however, the public accepted it, and it is the Gorsky version which has remained in the repertoire of the Bolshoi Theatre.

Gorsky remained as ballet master in Moscow until his death in 1924. He succeeded in vastly improving the calibre of the ballet company, which had been very low. His productions included a new version of Petipa's *The Daughter of Pharaoh* (Oct. 23, 1902), *Raymonda* (1908), *Giselle* (1911) and *Swan Lake* (1911). His innovations, which included the abandonment of strictly symmetrical patterns, and an increased dramatic expressiveness in the actual dancing, were gradually accepted. Gorsky's influence on the repertoire of the Bolshoi Theatre has remained very strong. He is credited with the choreography of current productions of *Swan Lake* (Acts I, II, and III), *Raymonda* (partly after Petipa), *The Little Hunchbacked Horse*, *Don Quixote* and *Coppélia*.

It is notable that Petipa never mentions the name of Michel Fokine. Neither in his violent diatribe against Gorsky, nor his calmer discussion of other choreographers does the old master mention the young one, who was just beginning his career. These Petipa memoirs were first published in 1906, but had probably been completed late in the preceding year. It was on April 8, 1906, that Petipa attended a performance of Fokine's little ballet *The Vine*, and sent the young choreographer a note which read: *"Cher Camarade, enchanté de votre composition, continuez et vous serez un grand maître de ballet."*

(7) Here Petipa, exasperated by what he considered Gorsky's desecration of two of his favourite works, *Don Quixote* and *The Daughter of Pharaoh*, has confused the two ballets himself. Commencing this sentence by mentioning *Don Quixote*, he concludes it with a reference to Aspicia, who is, of course, the protagonist in *The Daughter of Pharaoh*.

(8) Georgei Georgeivich Kyaksht, who had graduated from the Imperial Ballet School in St Petersburg in 1891, was the elder brother of Lydia Kyasht, who became so popular in London as the successor of Adeline Genée at the Empire Theatre. The name, in Russian, is properly *Kyaksht*, but was anglicized by Mme Kyasht at the time of her London début.

(9) Alexander Golovine (1864-1930) is best remembered for the exotic settings and costumes he designed for the original Diaghilev production of *The Firebird*, in 1910. At the time of which Petipa writes, he was a member of a group of *avant-garde* painters who were known as *les décadents*. Alexander Benois, a close friend and usually an admirer of Golovine's, shared Petipa's opinion of his settings for *The Magic Mirror*. He wrote in *The World of Art* (quoted in his *Reminiscences of the Russian Ballet*, p. 223): "There is much in Golovine's sets that is beautiful. But where is the ensemble? Where is the central idea? Everything seems so badly patched together, so little thought out ... His sets are like a very refined gastronomic dish, beside which our usual decor is no better than an ordinary *plat du jour*. And yet, in the theatre, these dull *plats du jour* are perhaps more in their place than a dish served at the wrong moment – however refined it may be."

(10) *The Magic Mirror*, first presented February 9, 1903, was an utter fiasco. It was received with whistles, cat-calls, and even shouts of "curtain". A vivid account of the disastrous performance is found in Yury Slonimsky's essay on Petipa, translated by Anatole Chujoy and published in *Dance Index*, Vol. VI, nos. 5 and 6, p. 126.

CHAPTER XIII

TROUBLES AND TRIBUTES

THERE now began a sad epoch, for our stage. The works of others are unceremoniously stolen or ruthlessly disfigured.

When *The Corsair* was produced for the benefit of Mlle Grantzova,[1] I had created for her a new *pas*, *Le Jardin animé*. The Moscow ballet master, Clustine,[2] staged this *pas* at his theatre, and had the audacity to call it his own, putting his name on the programme, knowing that I was still alive, thank God, and that I live in Petersburg.

M. Gorsky staged Perrot's *Esmeralda*, and Saint-Léon's *The Little Hunchbacked Horse* and *The Little Goldfish*, and my ballets *Don Quixote* and *The Daughter of Pharaoh*, and had the impertinence to cripple them and lower them in the estimation of the public, by meaningless innovations and changes.

Is it possible to demand that I acknowledge the merits of such ballet masters, and to accuse me of intrigues against talented competitors?

Indeed, I certainly did not plot against the really capable, competent, gifted late Lev Ivanov; I permitted him to choreograph ballets, and when we staged them together, always acknowledged his name on the programme. So, even as early as 1882, [actually 1893 – L.M.] we created and produced the ballet *Cinderella*; in 1887 we staged *The Tulip of Haarlem*, and in 1896 [i.e., 1895 – L.M.] the well-known ballet of Tschaikovsky, *Swan Lake*. In 1902 Lev Ivanov, following my scenario, staged alone and created all the dances for the ballet *The Nutcracker*, with music by Tschaikovsky.

As you see, I did not remove the really capable, competent, and talented ballet masters, or plot against them. On the contrary, I was always in very friendly relations with them, and was delighted to see in them persons capable of maintaining our ballet at its proper level.

Of the young choreographers, whom did M. Teliakovsky encourage when he removed me as too old? He sent his own ill-bred and ignorant adjutant, M. Krupensky, abroad to find a ballet master there. He brought here first a M. Coppini,[3] who did very little, and then a certain M. Berger,[4] whom Teliakovsky himself found it necessary to discharge at the first rehearsal, not letting him get beyond the first act.

And, indeed, did not M. Krupensky go abroad at State expense? And, indeed, were not Coppini and Berger brought to St Petersburg for nothing? On discharging them, it was necessary to pay a penalty for breach of contract. State money is spent freely, to allow M. Krupensky to rebuild the ballet in a new way. M. Teliakovsky has retained only one of the old customs: the Crown money is not spared, and the Crown bill is not reduced, in any experiment of his.

I can state that I created a ballet company of which everyone said: St Petersburg has the best ballet in Europe.

Being interested in the choreographic art, and loving my craft, I developed talented artists and showed them to the public, not just students without either knowledge or merit.

My works have appeared at almost every ballet performance, but they have not bothered to rehearse them, and my name has completely disappeared from the posters. Not long ago, in the ballet *Vain Precautions* (*La Fille mal Gardée*), Mlle Preobrajenska and Nicholas Legat danced a *pas de deux*, the creation of which was credited, on the programme, to M. Legat. In this *pas* they included my entire variation, and at the performance Mlle Preobrajenska had an enormous and well merited success.

Those acquainted with ballet affairs know that in any *pas*, the most difficult part to create is the variations, because it is necessary to give them a completely new character every time. One must attempt to avoid any resemblance to the

MARIUS PETIPA'S DAUGHTER, MARIE, WITH PAVEL GERDT
IN "THE SEASONS"

ALEXANDER GOLOVINE'S DESIGN FOR "THE MAGIC MIRROR",
ACT III, SCENE 6

MARIUS PETIPA, AGED NINETY

masses of other variations. My variations seemed suitable to M. Legat, but they forgot to put the name of the author in the programme. What will they do after my death? Then my name will never appear on the programme. In any case, it will disappear while M. Teliakovsky continues to manage the theatres, to their misfortune. M. Teliakovsky has diligently chased me off the programmes, just as he discarded my lezghinka in *Russlan and Ludmilla*.

But even now, the leading artists of the ballet come to me with requests to show them pantomimic scenes and create variations, which, of course, I always do with great pleasure. Not long ago the audience applauded Mlle Preobrajenska warmly when, with her usual talent and fire, she danced one such variation in the ballet *The Daughter of Pharaoh*.

At present, one hears of nothing but the quarrels and scandals among the members of the ballet troupe. Yet during my long career I always enjoyed the best relations with all the artists, and over this period there were many hundreds of them.

I did not please M. Teliakovsky, because I was willing to serve, but could not bring myself to fawn upon my superiors, but I always had the kindest consideration from Royalty, as well as the love of the public, my colleagues the ballet masters and composers, and all the dancers.

To avoid making an unsubstantiated statement, I will permit myself to give several more interesting letters.

Here is what M. Frolov, the Director of the Theatre School, wrote me after the production of the ballet *The Capricious Wife*:

"Dear Petipa,

I have just returned from the ballet, and before going to bed I want to congratulate you on your new victory. The Emperor expressed his warmest pleasure. It would have been impossible for things to go better, or with more enthusiasm. The children called forth general acclaim, and they danced together with a rare feeling of harmony. Sokolova and Gorshenkova appeared together as worthy competitors, and it is hard to say who won. In any event, you have the right to be proud of your new work. It is a pity that, unfortunately, you must lie in bed, although you are resting on laurels . . . I shake your hand with gratitude.

                                        Your friend,
                                             A. Frolov."

A letter from M. Rumine, also a head of the Theatre School, on August 5, 1888:

"Dear M. Petipa,
Wednesday we were so hurried with our departure that I was not able to see you in Gatchino after the performance. Therefore, I am obliged to resort to the aid of a pen, in order to tell you what enormous success your ballet divertissement had. His Majesty was delighted, and deigned to express his pleasure to me. Be assured of my gratitude, and believe in the sincere devotion of

                                        N. Rumine."

The well-known ballet master [actually, librettist – L.M.], Saint-Georges, writes to me on November 29, 1867:

"Dear Petipa,
This letter will be delivered to you by Mlle Grantzova, whose talent I literally adore. Mlle Grantzova has had a brilliant success in Paris in my ballet, *The Corsair*. She is not only a superb dancer, but a distinguished pantomimist.
Therefore, I recommend that you stage for her our charming ballet *Camargo*. You will never find a better performer, and then, I hope, I will see her in it in Paris, where you will stage it. I will be doubly excited: first, at seeing you again, and secondly, I am certain that my success will be divided with her, and with you. The best of wishes from your devoted

                                        Saint-Georges."

And here is another of his interesting letters:

"I have been assured that you are still in Petersburg, dear Marius, whereas, according to your last letter, I thought that you were already in Moscow. I hope that this letter will find you in Petersburg. Your news about your great success has made me extremely happy, and if I have not written you about it earlier, blame only my illness and weariness, moral as well as physical. I am overburdened with work, but I cannot, in any case, be unconcerned with your work and with you, whom I love so sincerely, and whose talent I admire. How happy I would be if I could be present at a performance of this wonderful ballet; I beg you to write me everything, down to the smallest details. I guarantee that I will read it with the most lively interest.

Write to me also about the ballerina and her success. Did our machinery and transformations work well? How did the elephant behave? Who will play and dance in our ballet in Moscow?

In Paris, the ballet is positively dead; in the entire season, they did not manage to stage anything. How sad this is, how painful. It is good that there are still foreign countries for people like me, who practice the cult of the choreographic art!

Please remind M. Gedeonov of my existence. With all my heart and soul, my dear collaborator,

Saint-Georges."

Five years later, on February 5, 1872, Mlle Grantzova wrote to me:

"Dear M. Petipa,

I am writing you these few lines to express my sincere gratitude for all the trouble and effort with which you taught me the role of Marguerite. Be assured that I will never forget either your good will, nor the personal kindness with which you treated me during this time. I permit myself to enclose
H

a small trifle, which I ask you to wear in memory of the sincere devotion and thanks of

Adéle Grantzova."

A letter from Mlle Grimaldi, from Moscow:

"Dear Master,

I am enclosing the programme of *The Corsair*. I send cordial greetings to you and your family.

Once again, from the depths of my heart, I thank you for your kindness to me during my débuts in Petersburg. Believe, please, in the deepest esteem of your

Enrichetta Grimaldi."

On the occasion of the production of the ballet *The Capricious Wife*:

"Dear Master,

This evening our choreographic stage will again be indebted to you for a triumph, and both of us are waiting happily to appear before the audience as remote but faithful echoes of your artistic genius. Receive, dear master, our sincere regret that we will not see you among us, and our hopes that we will soon be able to enjoy your incomparable advice.

With the assurance of our gratitude and sympathy, we send you these lines in memory of January 23, 1885. Your devoted

E. Sokolova, M. Gorshenkova."[6]

I will give a letter from the ballet regisseur, N. Aistov:

"Highly respected Marius Ivanovich!

Permit me to express to you, in the name of the entire corps de ballet, sincere gratitude for the benefit which, thanks to you, your work of artistic genius, and your renowned talent, had such an outstanding success. We may aspire to the highest artistic results, because you stand among us full-armed, ready for new labours and new sacrifices for the art dear to us.

N. Aistov, Regisseur of the Ballet."

In conclusion, a note from the composer Pugni,[7] March 23, 1860:

"Dear Marius,

I am sending you No. 2, the entrance of the Mother, No. 6, after the *grand pas*, No. 10, when the peasant comes to the aid of Stukolkin, No. 11, the entrance of the Burgomaster, No. 12, the entrance of the peasant men and women. I do not think a special entrance is necessary for the noblemen, they can come in during the finale of the twelfth number; the 13th number must be thrown out completely.

I tearfully ask you to send some money; I am without a penny. I am counting on finishing everything today.

Your friend,

Pugni.

PS. Don't you lose one little sheet, because I am sending you the drafts and I don't have any copies."

The above letters show how far I am from the portrait M. Teliakovsky has drawn of me, with his mean insinuations. M. Teliakovsky, who came to this business of ballet which was so completely strange to him! He behaved towards the arts as he did in the barracks and stables, from which he dared to come straight to the office of the Imperial Theatres.

I am grateful to him for only one thing: his disgusting behaviour induced me to put these memoirs in writing. I speak only the truth, which can be confirmed by documents as well as by witnesses.

It has been sad for me to see such a culmination to my career in Russia, where I have spent the best years of my life. With piety and devotion I recall the Court's relationship with me, and from my heart I thank the public and press of St Petersburg and Moscow for their constantly sympathetic reception, from which my creations and I myself have benefited.

And God bless my second fatherland, which I have learned to love with all my heart and with all my soul.

NOTES TO CHAPTER XIII

(1) Adèle Grantzova (or Grantzow, 1845-77) was a German dancer, the daughter of the ballet master at Brunswick. The choreographer Saint-Léon did much to further her career. In St Petersburg she danced *The Little Hunchbacked Horse*, *The Corsair*, *Giselle*, and many other ballets, creating the title roles in Petipa's *Trilby* and *Camargo*. A touching account of her short life (she died at thirty-two, after the amputation of a leg) appears in Ivor Guest's *The Ballet of the second Empire*, *1858-70*.

(2) Ivan Clustine (1862-1941) was trained in the Moscow school of the Imperial Theatres, where he graduated in 1878. After a brief tenure of the post of ballet master of the Bolshoi Theatre, he retired in 1903 in favour of the newly-appointed Alexander Gorsky. He was choreographer at the Paris Opéra, 1909-14, and then for many years travelled as ballet master with Anna Pavlova's company, arranging for her such works as *Amarilla*, *The Fairy Doll*, *Dionysus*, and *Snowflakes*.

(3) According to the *Annals of the Imperial Theatres*, Achille Coppini was employed as ballet master at the Maryinsky Theatre from August 1, 1902 to March 1, 1903. Son of a celebrated Italian choreographer, Antonio Coppini, Achille had been a solo dancer at La Scala, Milan, in 1882. Later he reproduced there a number of ballets by other choreographers, including Saint-Léon, Manzotti, Hassreiter, and his own father; but apparently he was not known for original choreography.

(4) Probably because of the hasty termination of his Russian engagement, the name of Berger does not appear in the *Annals of the Imperial Theatres*. In all probability, however, this was the same August Berger (1861-1945) who had staged the second act of *Swan Lake* in Prague in 1888 (see Chapter X, Note 7). Long active in Dresden and Prague, he was also assistant ballet master at the Metropolitan Opera, New York, under Rosina Galli, from 1922 to 1932.

(5) Enrichetta Grimaldi, noted for her technical virtuosity (like so many Italian ballerinas of her time), appeared as guest artist in St Petersburg in *Giselle*, *Coppélia*, *The Corsair*, and *The Sleeping Beauty*.

(6) Maria Nikolaevna Gorshenkova graduated from the Imperial Ballet School, St Petersburg, in 1876, and made her début as *Giselle*. Admired for her lightness and *ballon*, she later appeared in *Paquita, Satanella, Le Corsair, Don Quixote*, and *The Daughter of Pharaoh*.

(7) Cesare Pugni (1802-70), Italian composer noted for his facile and danceable ballet music, was educated at the Milan Conservatory of Music. He turned to ballet composition early in his career, and collaborated with such noted choreographers as Saint-Léon, Perrot, and Marius Petipa. His ballet scores include *Catarina, Esmeralda, Faust, The Daughter of Pharaoh*, and the famous *Pas de Quatre* danced in London in 1845, and so frequently revived in this century. Pugni worked in St Petersburg for nineteen years, from 1851 until his death.

BALLETS AND PRODUCTIONS BY MARIUS PETIPA, IN CHRONOLOGICAL ORDER

[Petipa's list contains a number of errors and omissions. Where possible, therefore, it has been checked and supplemented by other sources: Cyril W. Beaumont: *A History of Ballet in Russia*; Serge Lifar: *A History of Russian Ballet*; Alexander Plescheev: *Nash Balet*; Yury Slonimsky: *Marius Petipa*, translated by Anatole Chujoy; D. I. Leskhov: *Marius Petipa*; Lev G. Silvo: *Alphabetical Guide to the Ballet*. Where conflicting dates have been found, those given by Plescheev have been accepted in the majority of instances. Where works listed by Petipa have neither been confirmed nor contradicted, they have been accepted as he listed them.

It should be noted that the "principal performers" mentioned by Petipa did not always appear at the première, but sometimes interpreted leading roles in later productions. – L.M.]

1849   *The Swiss Milkmaid*. Music by Pugni. Principal dancer, Mlle Fanny Elssler.

1855   January 9. *L'Etoile de Grenade*. Divertissement.

1857   *The Butterfly, the Rose and the Violet*. Music by Prince Oldenburg. Staged in the open air, on the estate of His Highness Prince Oldenburg. Principal performers: Mme Petipa, Mlles Muravieva and Madaeva.

1858   December 18. *Un Mariage sous la Régence*. Music by Pugni.

1859   April 23. *The Parisian Market* (*Le Marché des Innocents*). Music by Pugni. Danced by Mme Petipa.

1859   *La Somnambule*. Music by Bellini. Principal dancer, Mlle Friedberg.

1860   April 30. *The Blue Dahlia*. Music by Pugni. Principal performers: Mme Petipa, and (in 1875, for her début) her daughter, Marie.

1861   November 15. *Terpsichore*. Divertissement, music by Pugni. Presented at Tsarkoïé Sélo, before the court.

95

1862   January 18. *The Daughter of Pharaoh*. Music by Pugni. Danced by Rosati (January 18) and Marie S. Petipa (October 4). This ballet had an enormous success and was given 208 performances.

1863   December 12. *The Beauty of Lebanon*. Music by Pugni.

1865   November 4. *The Travelling Dancer*. Music by Pugni. Theme, from a ballet by Philippe Taglioni. Principal performers, Mme Marie Petipa, Mlle Marie Petipa, Mlle Preobrajenska. [Note: The date of November 4, 1865, is given by Leskhov and Slonimsky. Silvo gives December 4, but agrees on 1865. Lifar places it in 1863, Petipa in 1869.]

1866   *Titania*. Ballet in one act. Music by Pugni. Danced by Mme Petipa. Staged in the Palace of the Grand Duchess Elena Pavlovna.

1866   January 20. *Florida*. Music by Pugni. Danced by Mme Petipa.

1868   April 27. *The Slave*. Divertissement, music by Pugni. Produced for a court spectacle.

1868   October 17. *Le Roi Candaule*. Music by Pugni. Principal dancer, Mlle Dor.

1869   December 14. One performance of the ballet *Don Quixote* in Moscow. Music by Minkus. Principal dancer, Mlle Sobechanskaya. Great success.

1870   January 20. *Trilby*. Music by Gerber. Produced in Moscow.

1871   January 17. First performance of *Trilby* in St Petersburg, for the benefit of Mlle Grantzova.

1871   January 31. *The Two Stars*, an Anacreontic ballet. Music by Pugni. For the benefit of Mlle Vazem, Mlle Vergina and M. Gerdt. The Stars: Mlles Vazem and Vergina. Apollo: M. Gerdt.

1871   November 9. First performance of *Don Quixote* in St Petersburg. Principal dancers, Alexandra Vergina (1871), Eugenia Sokolova (1874). Again a very great success.

1872   January 16. *La Péri*. Mlles Muravieva and Stanislavska.

1872   December 17. *Camargo*. Music by Minkus. Benefit of Mlle Adèle Grantzova.

1874 January 6. *Le Papillon*. Music by Minkus. Created by Saint-Georges and Petipa. Principal dancer, Mlle Vazem. Great success.

1875 January 26. *The Bandits*. Music by Minkus. Principal dancer, Mlle Vazem.

1876 January 18. *The Adventures of Peleus and Thétis*. Music by Delibes and Minkus. Principal dancer, Eugenia Sokolova. Great success.

1876 July 14. *A Midsummer Night's Dream*. Music by Mendels-sohn-Bartholdy. Staged at the Hermitage. Mlles Soko-lova, Marie Petipa, M. Gerdt.

1877 January 23. *La Bayadère*. Music by Minkus. Benefit of Mlle Vazem. Great success.

1878 January 29. *Roxana, or, The Beauty of Montenegro*. Music by Minkus. Benefit of Mlle Sokolova. His Majesty the Em-peror Alexander II liked this ballet very much, and honoured Petipa by praising his work very highly.

1878 *Ariadne*. Ballet staged in Moscow. Music by Gerber. Principal dancer, Mlle Sobechanskaya.

1879 January 7. *The Daughter of the Snow*. Music by Minkus. Mlle Vazem.

1879 March 11. *Frisac, the Barber, or, The Double Wedding*. Music by Minkus. Benefit of the corps de ballet.

1879 December 2. *Mlada*. Music by Minkus. Mlle E. Sokolova. Great success.

1880 February 24. *La Fille du Danube*. Music by Schneitzhoeffer. Benefit of Mlle Vazem.

1881 February 1. *Zoraya*. Music by Minkus. Benefit of Mlle Vazem. Great success.

1881 (?) *The Venetian Carnival*. Music by Paganini. *Pas de deux* danced by Mlle Ferraris and M. Petipa. [Note: It has not been possible to confirm this performance, and it seems most unlikely that it took place in 1881, since Mlle Ferraris retired in 1863 and Petipa, who was sixty-two years old in 1881, had not danced in public for some time. – L.M.]

1883 May 18. *Night and Day*. Staged in Moscow on the occasion of the coronation of His Majesty the Emperor Alexander III. Music by Minkus. Principal performers: Mlles Sokolova, Gorshenkova, Nikitina, and M. Johannsen.

1883 December 11. *Pygmalion.* Music by Prince Troubetzkoy. Principal dancers, Mlles Sokolova and L. Radina.

1886 February 9. *The Magic Pills*, a fairy tale. Music by Minkus. Great success.

1886 February 14. *The King's Decree.* Music by Albert Vizentini. Libretto by M. Gandinet. Principal dancer, Mlle Virginia Zucchi.

1886 July 22. *Les Offrandes à l'Amour.* Music by Minkus. Principal dancers, Mlles E. Sokolova and Marie Petipa.

1887 October 4. *The Tulip of Haarlem.* Music by Baron Schell. Staged by Petipa and Lev Ivanov. Principal dancer, Mlle Emma Bessone.

1888 February 17. *La Vestale.* Music by M. Ivanov. Libretto by M. Khudekov. Principal dancer, Mlle Elena Cornalba.

1889 January 25. *The Talisman.* Music by Drigo. Scenario by M. Tarnovsky and M. Petipa. Staging and dances by M. Petipa. For the benefit of Mlle Cornalba. Great success.

1889 June 5. *Les Caprices du Papillon.* Music by Krotkov. Principal dancers, Mlles Nikitina (1889) and Preobrajenska (1898). Great success.

1890 *The Grasshopper Musician.* Music by Krotkov. Principal dancer, Mlle Nikitina.

1890 January 3. *The Sleeping Beauty.* Music by P. Tschaikovsky. Principal dancer, Mlle Carlotta Brianza. Enormous success.

1890 November 11. *Nénuphar.* Music by Krotkov. Principal dancer, Mlle Brianza.

1891 February 13. *Kalkabrino.* Music by Minkus. Libretto by Modeste Tschaikovsky. Staging and dances by Petipa. Principal dancer, Mlle Brianza.

1892 January 10. *La Sylphide.* Ballet by Philippe Taglioni (father). Music by Schneitzhoeffer. Revision and staging by Petipa.

1892 June 12. *The Nutcracker.* Ballet in two acts and three scenes. Music by P. Tschaikovsky. Subject borrowed by

Petipa from *The Tales of Hoffman*. Staging and dances by L. Ivanov. Principal performers, Mlles Antonietta Dell'era (1892), Olag Preobrajenska (1900).

1893 *Cinderella*. Music by Baron Schell, Created by Marius Petipa and Lev Ivanov. Principal dancer, Pierina Legnani. [Note: The choreography of *Cinderella* is usually credited to Ivanov and Enrico Cecchetti. Possibly Petipa planned it, as he did *The Nutcracker*, also choreographed by Ivanov. – L.M.]

1894 July 28. *The Awakening of Flora*. Anacreontic ballet in one act. Music by Drigo. Principal performers, Mlles Kschessinska, Lubov Petipa, Pavlova, Vill, and Karsavina.

1895 January 15. *Swan Lake*. A fantastic ballet. Music by Tschaikovsky. Staged by Petipa and Ivanov. Principal performers, Mlles Legnani, Kschessinska, Preobrajenska. Very great success.

1896 January 21. *The Halt of the Cavalry*. Music by Armsheimer. Principal dancers, Mlles Legnani and Marie Petipa. Great success.

1896 May 17. *The Pearl*. Staged in Moscow for the coronation of His Majesty the Emperor Nicholas II. Music by Drigo. Principal dancer, Pierina Legnani. Great success.

1896 December 8. *Bluebeard*. Music by Schenk. Libretto by Pashkov. Principal performers, Mlles Legnani, Preobrajenska and Pavlova II.

1898 January 7. *Raymonda*. Music by Glazounov. Principal performers, Mlles Legnani and Preobrajenska.

1900 January 17. *Ruses d'Amour*. Ballet in the style of Watteau. Music by Glazounov. First performance at the Hermitage, January 17; at the Maryinsky Theatre, February 13. Principal performers, Mlles Legnani, Kulishevskaya, Marie Petipa, Lubov Petipa, Nadejda Petipa.

1900 February 7. *The Four Seasons*. Music by Glazounov. First performance at the Hermitage, February 7; at the Maryinsky Theatre, February 13. Principal dancer, Mlle Kschessinska.

1900   February 10. *Harlequinade*. Music by Drigo. First performance at the Hermitage, February 10; at the Maryinsky
Theatre, February 13. Principal performers, Mlles Kschessinska and Preobrajenska. Great success.

1900   February 17. *Les Elèves de M. Dupré* (a shortened version
of *The King's Decree*). Music by A. Vizentini, Delibes, and
others. Principal performers, Mlles Legnani and Kschessinska.

1900   February 23. First performance in St Petersburg of *The
Pearl*.

1903   February 9. *The Magic Mirror*. Music by Koreschenko.
Principal dancers: Mlles Kschessinska, Preobrajenska,
Marie Petipa.

1903   *King Sing*. Ballet not yet produced.

1904   *The Romance of the Rose and the Butterfly*. Music by Drigo.
Libretto by M. V——. Ballet prepared for presentation
the Hermitage in 1904, but not yet produced.

REVIVALS AND PRODUCTIONS OF FOREIGN BALLETS, STAGED BY MARIUS PETIPA

1847   *Catarina.* Music by Pugni. Created by Perrot. Principal dancer, Mlle Fanny Elssler.

1847   *Paquita.* Created by Foucher and Mazilier. Principal dancer, Mlle Andreyanova.

1848   *Satanella.* Staged in Moscow for Mlle Andreyanova.

1850   *Giselle.* Music by Adam. Principal dancer, Carlotta Grisi. Great success.

1850   *The Naiade (Ondine).* Music by Pugni. Created by Perrot. Principal dancer, Carlotta Grisi. Great success.

1867   *Faust.* Music by Pugni. Created by Perrot. Principal dancer, Wilhelmina Salvioni. Great success.

1867   *La Vivandière.* Music by Pugni. Created by Saint-Léon. Principal dancer, Mlle Salvioni.

1867   *The Goldfish.* Music by Markus. Created by Saint-Léon. Principal dancer, Mlle Salvioni.

1868   *L'Amour bienfaiteur.* Staged in the Theatrical School. Principal dancer, the student Sokolova.

1868   January 25. *The Corsair.* Created by Saint-Georges and Mazilier, after the story by Lord Byron. Music by Adam, Pugni, and others. Staging and new dances created by Petipa. For the benefit of Mlle Grantzova.

1868   *The Little Hunchbacked Horse.* Created by Saint-Léon. Music by Pugni. Principal dancers, Mlles Muravieva and Vazem. Great success.

1870   *Satanella.* Staged in St Petersburg for Mlle Vergina.

1884   *Coppélia.* Music by Delibes. Principal dancer, Mlle Nikitina.

1885   January 23. *Le Diable à Quatre (The Capricious Wife).* Benefit of Mlles Sokolova and Gorshenkova. In the last act all the new dances had a huge success.

1885   *Vain Precautions (La Fille mal Gardée).* Created by Dauberval. Principal performers, Mlles Virginia Zucchi, Kschessinska, Preobrajenska, Vinogradova.

1886   *Esmeralda*. Created by Perrot. New *Pas de Six* created by M. Petipa, for the benefit of Mlle Zucchi. Performed also by Mlle Kschessinska. Great success.

1887   *Fiametta*. Music by Minkus. Created by Saint-Léon. Principal performers, Mlles Kschessinska and Vinogradova.

DANCES STAGED BY MARIUS PETIPA IN OPERAS

1856   *Le Dieu et la Bayadère.* Tenor: Tamberlik. Dancer: Zina
       Richard.

1872
1881   } *Oberon.*

1874
1880   } *Hamlet* (Ballet: *La Fête du Printemps*). Success.

1874   *Roussalka.*

1874   *Russlan and Ludmilla.* Lezghinka danced by Marie Petipa
1886   and M. Bekefi. Encored every time.

1875   *Aida.*

1879
1884   } *Rogneda.*

1879   *Il Guarany,* an Indian opera [i.e., Brazilian – L.M.].

1880   *The Queen of Sheba.*

1881
1885   } *Mephistopheles.*

1881   *Le Roi de Lahore.*

1883   *Philemon and Baucis.* Dances repeated three times.

1883   *L'Étoile du Nord.*

1883   *Orpheus in the Underworld.* After the dances, M. Petipa was
       called out.

1883   *Richard III.*

1883   *La Gioconda.* Dance of the Hours; ovation and encore.

1884   *Aldona.*

1884   *Lalla Rookh. Pas de Cachemires*; great success.

1884   *Nero.*

1884
1886   } *The Demon.* Lezghinka always encored.

1887   *Manon.* The management, as well as the public, was de-
1897   lighted with all the period dances.

1897   *Hänsel and Gretel.* The tableau of the angels had enormous
       success.

1897   *The Tales of Hoffmann.*

1898   *Don Giovanni.*
1898   *Feramors (Lalla Rookh).*
1899   *Faust.* The Walpurgis night ballet had a very great success.
1899   *Les Huguenots.* Dances encored.
1899   *Robert le Diable.*
1899   *L'Africana.*
1899   *Tannhäuser.*
1900   *The Queen of Spades.*
1900   *Carmen.* Marie Petipa danced *El Olé* with enormous success.
1900   *Le Prophête.*
1900   *Fra Diavolo.*